A
Single
Tear

A Single Tear

Jamae Vandegraph

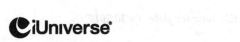

A SINGLE TEAR

iUniverse books may be ordered through booksellers or by contacting:

iUniverse
1663 Liberty Drive
Bloomington, IN 47403
www.iuniverse.com
1-800-Authors (1-800-288-4677)

ISBN: 978-1-5320-6936-9 (sc)
ISBN: 978-1-5320-6935-2 (e)

Library of Congress Control Number: 2019903419

Print information available on the last page.

iUniverse rev. date: 04/30/2019

This is my story being told through words and poetry. My story began when I was only six years old. I lived with my parents and five brothers. We lived in a nice quiet neighborhood in a two story home that was built by my father and grandfather. Our neighborhood consisted of mostly the older generation so it was a pretty quiet neighborhood with immaculate yards and flower gardens. Life at that time was pretty good; your usual teasing by brothers to a sister, riding bicycles and chasing fireflies in the evening. We had a relatively normal childhood. We spent most of our time outside playing and chasing each other and climbing trees, and yes sneaking off to play in the creek. We ate supper together at the table and after dark we enjoyed catching lightning bugs. As children we had a variety of pets come in and out of our lives and one in particular was our dog Leader. Leader was a guard dog who stayed outside on a long run which my dad constructed out of thick cable attached to a tree at one end and was attached to the outside corner of the garage at the other end. Then Leader's chain was attached to a pulley that ran up and down the cable. Leader was a black and dark brown medium sized mixed breed dog that was as sweet as can be with us but would attack anyone trying to break into dad's garage. Dad's garage was pretty much what today's dads now call a "man cave." My dad wasn't a big man but normal in height and medium build and he spent most of his free hours in this garage either by himself or on a regular basis, his racing buddies would drop by, have a beer and visit over working on the race car. I spent quite a bit of time sitting and just petting that old dog and admiring my dad and this race car that he built with his own two hands with only the body of an old Coop. This race car won many races and had changed in color throughout the years and eventually was sold for a long rail body race car as dad was getting older and needed a car with less of a vibration. I spent even more time with Leader telling him all my horrible secrets after my life changed for the worse. I don't know how or who first met the man with a heart of steel but this stranger who moved into the big three story old house a block away from us didn't waste any time getting to know my family. Two to three times a week this horrible new neighbor would call our house and ask my mother if my brother and I could come over and help him unpack his priceless treasures. I don't know about you but if these treasures were so priceless why on earth would you want two small children touching them? The treasures were antiques but looked like old junk to me. This man would phone my mom and ask her to send us to his house. My mom was told he needed us to help him unpack or sort through his numerous items he collected for his home business. His collection consisted of older items and unusual one of a kind types of "knick knacks" I guess you would call them. Back then in the 60's and early 70's parents didn't have to worry about child predators; it was unheard of in our small town. But one managed to move in a block away. I don't recall helping to unpack anything. I don't even recall how or what he did with my brother; I do know we were always separated some how. I just know I always left that old house alone and hurting, not just physically but emotionally and confused. I was always told by this man that my mom asked him to teach me to be a good young lady and if I told anyone I would be in big trouble and my dad would take a belt to me. Now as an adult I know these were all lies. But as a scared little girl you believe every word an adult would say to you. He prepped me day after day for the "big special day" as he called it. It started out as playing hide and seek with an object like a small ball or a quarter that he would hide in his pocket then down his pants and I would have to find it, then it was my turn and after a few times playing this game he decided to show me a better place to hide things. This game for me was no longer fun but becoming quite scary. I was also shown a book of children in different compromising positions in hopes it would extinguish any questions I might have lingering in the back of my mind that this was wrong. I now know that this horrible book was a book of child pornography and I feel horrible for those children. These pictures and games are still so vivid in my mind. I remember he would take me upstairs to a corner bedroom that was always dark and cold, with no furniture. I do remember there was an old wooden tripod with a big camera that rested on its top; this room was not so inviting or pretty to a little girl's eye. Here is where I was always unclothed and he too would remove his clothing and the games became real and much scarier, with him touching me and him forcing me to touch him by him placing his hands on mine and forcing this touch upon me. If anyone would come knocking on the front door I was forced into a small closet, usually naked and told to be quiet or else. I was scared, cold and alone. I would just curl up in the fetal position and close my eyes and pray to be back at home. I always wondered where my brother was. I never quite understood where he always disappeared to and to this day I still wonder and still have no answer. We always came to this big scary house together, but I always left alone. This man was married when we met him but later on his wife left him and today I know in my heart she left him knowing what he was doing to me. I always wanted to ask her why she never told the authorities. Why she never helped me. I do know I will never get answers from her or anyone. I don't remember anything about her. I still tell myself someday I will approach this monster of a man when I'm in Illinois and I will tell him what he has taken from me and I will have my questions answered and also have my say. I know it can never be dealt with in the court room but it will be done. I feel he owes me at least a few minutes of his time to answer questions. I need to tell him he is a horrible person and what he has done or is possibly still doing will cost him in the end. I want him to know all I have endured throughout my life and all I have overcome. He needs to see I am a survivor and I know when my time on earth is over I will not have to worry about seeing him in heaven. I am not just a survivor but I have used my horrible experiences for good. As an EMT I use my past to see through the wall that is put up to hide the hurt and pain that is living inside too many of my patients. When I get a young patient who has been abused I tell her that I am not perfect; that I was hurt too and that helps them to feel safe and comfortable enough with me to remove part of this wall and to open up to me so I can help them get just the right type of help they deserve and need. The more they open up to me the more I can document and pray this will help them get the help they need at this time. I wish I could have had someone like me to help me when I needed to be saved. I only had Leader and at that time in my life Leader was my EMT. When I needed a place to hide from the world his dog house was my refuge. We all have some kind of hurt in us whether it is sexual, physical, or emotional; something as little as losing your pet goldfish and a family member flushing it down the toilet when you wanted it buried. That is a type of hurt that may seem petty to some; but to a child it isn't petty because you truly loved this fish with your heart and it hurt to lose it. So you see we all have been hurt or felt pain at one time or other in our lives. If we didn't we would not be human. GOD gave us emotions and feelings to use and to learn from, not to bury them and be cold and heartless uncaring people. I am ok with sharing my story with the world because I hope I can further heal by writing it and others can read it and know there is a life out there for us who have been hurt. Life is just waiting for us to take charge and make it ours. We are the only ones who can change to make us happy and free.

I started writing poetry when I was in my thirties. Writing was a means for me to put my feelings on paper and to visualize the anger and nightmare that lives inside of me. I experienced a lot of hurt in a very short amount of time in my life. Being the young victim of a child molester was hard enough to live with. And then knowing my face, my young nude body was also out there in a book of pornography just like those children I saw in that book this man had. This was hard to swallow and I was praying this hurt would end with me moving away from this neighborhood. As a child you only think about the now and think everyone is good. I thought once we moved out of this house and away from here then I would be safe and there would be no more hurt. I never thought there could be more people just like this man out there; after all isn't he the only bad man? While visiting my grandmother, all of us, myself and five brothers and any other children at Grandma's that day, would walk up the block to the park to play. I found myself at the end of the day playing at the park alone, realizing my brothers had all left and went back to Grandma's. I don't remember how I managed to meet up with these two older teenage boys but somehow I found myself in the right place for them but the wrong place for me. They coaxed me or forced me, I don't remember those details, but I remember being in the back seat of this car and one of the teen boys forcing himself on top of and inside me and how it hurt and shocked me. I laid there crying on that back seat afraid to move or talk. Then the boy behind the steering wheel who had been driving told the boy who was on top of me that there was a "cop" coming down the road. Next thing I knew the car sped off and dumped me next to some bushes by my grandmother's house. Not only was I relieved to be at my Grandma's but relieved to be away from those boys. I was scared and confused what just happened to me but also about why this happened. So many questions lurked in my head. Did anyone see what just took place? After all, all here were my brothers running around playing in the yard. Do they know that I was just tossed out of that car? If they did, why aren't they concerned and running over to me? I did not know about rape at that age but here I was laying on the ground and a victim of rape. Here I was once again telling my secrets to an animal, this time it was Momma Kitty, my grandma's old cat. She was a grey tiger striped smaller framed cat who had a litter of kittens at least twice a year and lived to be thirty two years old. Grandma's old cat outlived Grandma herself. This love I had for animals was starting to become my therapy, so to speak. I was slowly losing my trust in humans and found myself alone most of the time or being teased and tormented by my brothers, so at this stage in life I felt being alone was safer. The divorce of my parents was especially hard on me. It was tough and confusing. I believe most of the confusion lied in the fact that my mom's best friend and our next door neighbor is now my step mother. This explained why I witnessed my dad kissing the neighbor lady one evening. This was an emotional time for all of us kids but witnessing what I saw was always in the back of my mind. My five brothers and I were separated as I feared would happen. My three stepbrothers and some of my brothers at times live with my dad in another state. I just could not comprehend that, another state? I will never see them again; it is too far to ride a bicycle to another state. This is all my 9 year old brain could think of. After my parents' divorce I lived with my mother. She did not have it easy at all; she had to learn first of all how to drive, and then learn how to work outside the home and get a place for us to live and how to just survive. During these first few years my mom had met different guys she dated and started drinking to hide her pain. Life was hard for my mom; she had no help to find direction in her life. As I was turning into a preteen, mom met and started dating a nice guy who I eventually grew to accept and I thought he was cool at times; I guess it all depended on my mood; I was after all turning into a very resentful and angry pre-teen. I stayed very reserved and would rather be with my friends who I trusted and not be around any older people, such as adults. I will never forget my 13th birthday; it wasn't your typical glamorous becoming a teenager birthday party but just the opposite. My mom and this man I sometimes called "dad" took me out to dinner and gave me my birthday gift, I still have this gift today, and it was nice and I did feel special. But they had also made previous arrangements for their own night out but arranged for the younger brother of this man I sometimes call "dad" to come over and sit with me and watch TV or movies so I wouldn't have to spend my birthday alone. This guy was way younger than "dad" and was just a few years older than me and yes I did have a little girl crush on him and was so excited he actually chose to be here with me instead of with his own girl friend. What started out as an ok evening ended in a nightmare. He had been drinking and decided he would have his way with me too. I was shocked at his actions and begged him "don't do this, please stop" but all my begging fell upon deaf ears. I never told my mom, at least not that night or the next day. But after a month and no period I knew I had to tell but how? I was so afraid and felt I was going to be in such big trouble. All I could think about was how do I approach her, do I ask her to sit down do I tell her through the bathroom door while she is on the toilet? Yes that would be safest then I can run out the door before she gets done. I finally chose to ask her while we were fixing supper together. I gathered up all my strength hung my head and just told her. "Mom, I was raped by "Dad's" brother the night of my birthday and now I am pregnant. Whew! That was easier than I thought… now the reaction. But to my astonishment there was no bad reaction; I think mom was just as shocked at hearing this as I was going through the rape. Yes, now I was old enough to know I was raped. Mom and I sat down and discussed making a clinic appointment to find out for sure and we would go from there to make a plan. The plan turned out not in my favor as I saw it. Yes, I was pregnant but with my age and small size and the history of drug use and alcohol use by this guy my doctor felt I should abort the fetus. I was so torn but I had no say in this matter; after all I was only 13. My mom was so hurt not only for me but for her relationship and what her life style had turned into. This was just what my mom needed to wake up and clear her head and change. I was surprised by her decision to not marry this guy after what his brother had done to me. I could not believe that I mattered in the decision as big as that; maybe I am loved and maybe I do matter. But as a teen I pushed that aside and only felt the hurt, shame, and the pain I knew I caused myself and my family. What really hurt the most was hearing my very own grandmother tell me how disappointed in me she was. She told me I was just out there spreading my legs and killing GODS children. Those words have never left my brain. I never told anyone and it has never been mentioned and those words have never affected the way I feel about my grandma, because I knew GOD knows the truth. Life for me after that would get worse, oh yes worse. As a teenager I was in and out of foster homes and one group home where I was once again raped at the age of 15. So by the time I eventually ended up the ward of the state I was doing a lot of thinking and getting more and more withdrawn from my own family. What really hurt the most was I felt being the only girl I was unwanted. After all, everybody had their home with mom or dad or by this time the older boys living in their own homes, but here I was in a strange place surrounded by kids and adults I don't even know and terrified to fall asleep. The dark was a very scary place for me now so I became very frightened when those lights would be turned out. And then there was my baby brother living so far away with my dad; I missed him the most, but I missed everybody so much. I wished I could see my family, my grandma and grandpa but I knew I must have been a really bad kid to end up here and I was. I had a very hard time seeing my mom struggle every day and having to move from place to place. To me, I was just another burden and should just disappear. I got to the point I didn't want to see her struggle like that anymore so the older I got the more I started acting out and staying away. I would spend the night with what friend or brother would have me that night. Little did I know at that time I was making life harder for my mom. And it was at that point I was considered the ward of the state and was placed in homes and finally that group home. After a couple years my mom finally found a great job she loved and met the right man, the man who would become my stepfather and life was so much happier and easier for her after that. But my life was still unchanged for a couple more years. As I grew older I went to seek help through state run services and slowly began to heal. Part of that healing was to write down my feelings or put my feelings together into a poem. Writing poetry never came easy for me. I am not one to just sit down and write. My poems, you could say, come to me at different times. Sometimes in the middle of the night I will wake up and write down words which don't make sense at that time but eventually the rest of the words follow along and the words become a poem. Most of my poems are about anger and hurt, but one day I wrote my first heartfelt poem for my stepdad after his beloved cat "Stubby "passed away. This is when I realized I could write poems that would help ease the pain from the loss of a loved one. Writing, I found, if not for any particular person but rather for yourself, was a much better solution for getting your thoughts across, than committing suicide. I hope that if just one person reads my book and thinks "maybe I will try this instead of suicide" then this book will be worth it. We have so many young people out here in my part of the world who are talented and take their own lives. They are full of anger and hurt and have the illusion there is nothing out there in this world for them. Some don't think or rationalize how this one act, in the moment of pain or anger, will have a lifetime effect on all involved. I had those same thoughts. I have no talent and I'm just an average person but I found what works for me. I hope you find what works for you. This is a big world and there's something and someone for everyone, just don't ever give up looking. The first poem is of my bad experience at the park when I was nine years old, the second poem is for my stepdad and the difference between the two is so remarkable. You will notice the difference in my time of healing between the two poems. One poem I was still in the hurting stages and this was all I could see. By the second one I was finally able to break out of my shell and feel something other than hate or anger; I was now feeling sympathy for someone I loved. I always had these positive feelings but they rarely surfaced except for when I had my first child. He was innocent just as I was and I was now needed.

A Single Tear

There were two of them
And just 9 year old –me
They would have their way
And did as they pleased
One was the look-out
While the other played
Two teenage boys
Getting a thrill for the day
The look-out would watch
For the big boss man
The one with a badge
And a gun in his hand
In the back seat I was held down
So no one could see
This little girl from town
As I laid there scared and afraid
A single tear had broken away
Quickly I just brushed it free
For no one can witness
this weaker side of me
as an officer rounded his final block
the lookout hollered here come the cops
One block two blocks we had driven
The door was then opened
a push I was given
I landed in the bushes
near my grandma's house

here I just sat
quiet as a mouse
I finally ran to
the back porch door
Inside I sat on the
Kitty litter strewn floor
then something soft began
Rubbing against my fore arm
She made her way round
My lap she was looking for
To her this spot was quite appealing
Her soft purring and love
was just the right type of healing
As a tear rolled down my dirtied cheek
I wiped it off on MaMa Kitty's fur so sleek
I whispered in her ear
No one could ever know
For what just happened
I shall never speak

To Dad With Love

I came to you as a small kitten astray
A home I found, with you I would stay
A tail I hadn't one, for it was missing
So the name you gave me was quite fitting
This name that was chosen for me was Stubby
Right away I knew you would be my best buddy
I grew and I grew to a whopping 22 pounds
You wondered how this could be
That same kitten we found
With plenty of attention and lots of love
It's no wonder the good LORD sent me from above
He knew there was something missing in your home
So that void I came to fill
No longer will I roam
I had a friend in need of a home too
This is why I brought in Two Foot for you
You were two humans in need of a pet
With Two Foot and I
Your needs had been met
We had it all planned, yes just we two
Two homeless kittens who found
A home and love with you
We romped and we played
We terrorized the place
We knew we were in trouble
By the looks upon your face
You bought us toys to play with

Whenever we were left alone
But we preferred yours
When you weren't at home
We were never thrown out,
Beaten, abused, or hurt
Just a scolding or two
Sometimes a cuss word you would blurt
A couple of years have passed
No longer are we kittens
We are now teenagers looking for adventure
But trouble is all we are getting
We did find time for you
To pet us and be rubbed
Even with our adventures
We knew we were loved
As we've grown older
We have slowed down quite a bit
The only ones quick moving
Are the grandchildren Shar has bit
My time is growing short
No longer can I stay
But just around the corner
Is another homeless stray
I am very sorry but I must leave you now
I hope you will take in others
and love them too somehow
The good LORD is calling
So I must go you see
For Grandpa and Grandma are waiting
For me to lie upon their knee
This isn't good-by

It's just so long for now
I shall take my once and final bow
I have loved you so much
You are my best buddy
I will miss you always
And thank you — LOVE STUBBY

As a little girl I made a good friend, whose name was Brandi who moved just up the block from me. She was the younger of two girls, her older sister was high school age and she thought she was way too cool for us. Both her parents were college professors and were always home when she came home from school. I spent a lot of time over at her house playing. Brandi, had the best swing set and teeter-totter and yard and a great big beautiful Golden Retriever. All the kids in the neighborhood played at Brandi's house. We would act out plays and put on a show for the college students who lived in the apartments behind Brandi's house. When we got a little older we went into gymnastics and her parents purchased a set of uneven bars for us to use in the back yard. Her dad set them up and helped us while we used them; we were never allowed to use them unless an adult was there to spot us and we had such a great time. When Brandi and her family would go on vacation I was always with them. They thought of me as a third child. Brandi and I did brownie scouts together and went to summer camps. We were like sisters. We fought and argued just like sisters but we never stayed mad at each other for very long. Being a child at that time was fun and easy. We kept busy using our imaginations and role playing. Bicycles turned into horses and sticks were guns or swords. It was all fun and innocent. At one point her parents were asking to adopt me after my parents divorced. I really loved her parents; her mom was always so great with us when we wanted to play dress up. She had this big box full of neat scarves and boas and dresses with shiny sequins on them. We always had something fun to do at her house. I always wished we could do the same at my house. Her parents were so hands on and had more time than my parents. I guess with six kids versus two kids my parents had their hands full and probably had a lot less time to play dress up or whatever games we played. As a child this just doesn't come into your rational thought system I guess. Having that special bond with my girlfriend and her parents did give me a life time of wonderful memories. I love them for allowing me to be a part of their family when I was in need of this special kind of love and belonging in my life. It was a struggle for me after my parents divorced and we moved away. I really missed Brandi and that special bond we had. I also missed the safety net I had at their home. I felt secure with her parents and them checking on us to see if we were where we should be. My folks kept an eye on us but it wasn't the same. We weren't bad kids but we were naturally curious as kids. I love my mom and dad dearly and they are awesome parents and did a great job with all of us kids. My dad spent most of his time at work and afterwards in the garage working on his race car. We would see him if we went to the garage. But it was just a fact and given that the garage was not a place to play. We would go and ask questions about the race car and he would show us things and explain how it ran. But that would be a short visit; after all we had other adventures to conquer. My dad was always my hero as a child growing up; he built his own race car and won many trophies. To a child that was cool. But having a dad who would hug me and call me his little princess like Brandi's dad did with her, this is what I wanted too and longed for. My son Brandon who is grown and has children of his own is that type of father. I watch him with his children and he will dance to a song with my granddaughters standing on his shoes and he calls them princess. Brandon is great with both his sons too. Those boys are right there with him helping with car repairs or playing basketball. Just planting flowers in the yard is a family project. I am so proud of my son; he coaches baseball and football and is that kind of father that Brandi had. I am missing out on so much of my son's life with his children living in a different state and it hurts to know this, but at the same time I could not stay in Illinois and heal. I tried and there is nothing there for me. My family means the world to me, but I am in the place where I need to be. I still wonder what I could have had done different to be my daddy's little girl. Out of that I wrote these poems.

Daddy's Girl

If I could have been a daddy's girl
I might have grown up in a safer world
I should have been a ballerina
Holding daddy's hand as I twirled
I would have helped him in his garage
We could have together fixed his fast race car
I could have been his special pit crew
I would hand him the tools that he would use
If only I could have been a daddy's girl
I would not of had grown up in that monsters world
That monster he came calling for me
in his house I was scared as can be
If daddy had known I'd been safe at home
With my brothers climbing trees
But that would not be the fate for me
I could have been coloring or reading a book
The monsters stories had a whole different look
The monster played very different games than we
His games were scary and hurt parts of me
He would hide me in the closet without my clothes on
if anyone would come knocking on his door
Where is my dad please come with mom
I would cry lying on that hard cold floor
Why won't my daddy come rescue me
I hate this monster can't my family see
Why can't I be a daddy's girl

Why can't I live in my dream world
Why do these monsters even exist
Can't anyone get this problem fixed
If only I were a daddy's girl

The Golden Cup

Tall and slender and quite the man
With a heart filled with love
He works towards his plan
He works real hard
Pouring hot molten Steele
Working long hot hard hours
And that's for real
When not at work
To school he must go
To earn that degree
Before the doors close
A better life for his family
Is what he is after
At times he misses out
On hearing his children's laughter
This young man's life
Has always been hard
But giving up has never
Been in his deck of cards
He pulls himself together
And moves right along
With GOD by his side
He continues to stay strong
He coaches football in winter
And baseball all summer
Coaching these children
is never a bummer

with dance recitals and cheer practice too
not to mention school plays
and clinic waiting rooms
he gets very little sleep
but knows he can't give up
because a better future
is his golden cup
this young man I write about
is too my pride and joy
I could never be more proud
Is my first baby boy

When I first met my current husband I was going through a bitter divorce and ending ten years in an unsuccessful marriage. There was some physical abuse but that was not near as damaging as the mental and emotional abuse. Some people see the bruises on the face of an abused woman and think "oh, he beats his wife how horrible" but they never stop to think how much damage the mental and emotional abuse can cause. The bruises, well, they go away after a few days but long term emotional abuse stays with you a life time. This is just a small part of what I am overcoming. I think what has hurt me the most in my marriage was the part when my ex husband would get my boys to play along with him in his game to torment me. It was a game to him but for me it was torture and I knew the boys didn't know any better. After a few years of that kind of mental abuse I think boredom set in because the physical abuse started, not just on me but also on my oldest son. When the physical abuse occurred to my oldest boy I sent him to a friend's home at first to keep him safe. I felt he would be close and I would see him often and he could come home when he was not in school and on weekends until I could get through my divorce. When it was parent teacher conference time for my oldest son I drove to the school where he was now attending just to be informed I was not allowed to partake in the conferences because I had abused my son. I was floored, speechless and felt horrified at how this could happen. It took a few phone calls to a social worker and for her to send paper work with the truth. I felt so betrayed. I could only look at all these people, so many teachers and parents staring at me. I know they all heard what this one principal had said, "I abused my son". I kept asking myself "how can this all be undone"? Why is this being said in front of all these people? I never touched my son to hurt him or even to discipline him nor would I ever. All these people staring at me thinking I hurt my son. This school took the word of someone; I don't even know who told them this. Was it my "soon to be" ex-husband? Why did they believe that I abused my son instead of talking to me or social services? The school called to apologize for their short comings but the damage was done and there was no way for all those parents and teachers and students to un-hear that "I abused my son". My son came home with me on that day and we decided to drive to Illinois to get him settled in with his Nanny. At least this way I was involved in all the decisions and there was no lying about why he was in one state and I living in another. After getting my son settled I came back home and started working at a local diner as a waitress. One afternoon this stranger came into the diner and I had no clue this man, who I never had seen before, would be the change in my life I now know I deserved. After seeing this stranger that one afternoon he came into the diner quite often to eat. He and the owners were good friends and had known each other for years. We were introduced and things just grew from there. I had several horses and had lost some property I used for my horses to graze on and I also used half of this property to cut hay for the winter months. It was, I guess really no surprise I lost the land, it did belong to my ex husbands family. So I was looking for a way to earn some pasture or hay bales to keep my horses fed. I was told the guy who comes into the diner now quite frequently had land and maybe I could work for him part time to pay for rent or hay. So we were introduced and it was agreed I would fix fence and help feed cows and in exchange I could keep my horses out to his place. Little did I know how hard the work was or how hard I would fall in love with this most wonderful man. We started dating after a few months. I eventually sold my house after about a year later and then my children and I moved out to the ranch so Carl and I could see more of each other. We both knew I came from abuse and we decided we would tackle that together if we were to ever make our relationship work. We started therapy for me and my son; we also went to family counseling. My oldest son decided he would like to stay with his Nanny and finish school so I let him stay in Illinois with the knowledge our home was his home. He was in his teens and he was a big help to his Nanny, so it worked for them both. He sought counseling in Illinois and did come home to visit several times. He is now grateful for that time he had with his Nanny before she passed away. I was happy he was such a big help while she was alive and he was kept safe and was healing at the same time. Now it was my turn and my youngest son's turn for healing. I needed to learn to trust and live with a man who was not abusive and my new male friend needed to learn how to live with and help an abused woman. My son, he needed to learn how to be a child and live without chaos. It's not a quick fix; it took a few years and it is a continual process. I was a broken woman and I felt every day this would be the day I was going to lose the one perfect man in my life. I explained how I felt and admitted I was having a hard time with him being around his female friends. We both agreed to keep them at a distance till I felt more comfortable. I felt horrible much of the time just knowing how much time and effort had to be put in just to live with me. We had bad days and a few horrible days but finally we had good days and they were starting to outweigh the horrible and bad days. I was taught to run the Ranch and farm equipment and found it was really peaceful working out in the fields. I found it was not only peaceful but also relaxing. The time apart from each other while working in the fields helped to bring us closer together. Between counseling and keeping busy I started to trust again and I was too busy to have bad thoughts. I learned I was making Carl pay for all the bad that had happened in my marriage. Here sits this wonderful guy who didn't deserve a bit of my accusations and I was putting him through a life of hell. I am ever so grateful this man had so much time and love for me that he was willing to fight my demons to keep me. As I started to learn how to cope and live a "normal" life I was starting to write more poems and I would write Carl letters in forms of poems to express myself easier. It was really hard to talk about my feelings to any one, especially Carl. Talking to my therapist took a very long time just to open up and feel comfortable enough to talk about certain subjects. So as far as Carl went, writing came easier for me and I didn't have to talk face to face on different subjects or a disagreement. I was very fearful of upsetting Carl. I feared I would be struck or left homeless if I upset him; after all I sold my home and was now living in his. This was a major step for me so I did a lot of writing and it finally came to the point to where we could communicate anything face to face. This is one poem I wrote during my non face to face communications to Carl on the female friends' subject. I look back at it now and tell myself how silly I was to think like that. We love each other and true love is a strong bond not easily broken.

Plain Ole Me

I'm not big and strong or know
Everything about cows like Donna
I'm just plain ole me
This is the way I will always be
I'm not beautiful or blond or have
A college degree like Vicky
I'm just plain ole me
This is the way I will always be
I no longer own land or have
A good paying respectable job like Peggy
I'm just plain ole me
This is the way I will always be
I don't own my own business or have
Many talents or child free like Shelly
I'm just plain ole me
This is the way I will always be
I'm not pretty and skinny or
An EMT like Natalie
I'm just plain ole me
This is the way I will always be

But

I never saw, not a single one
Take your hand in marriage or
Commit to help you in this ranch to run
I cook your meals and clean your house
I help round up all your cows
I sort them out and do the feeding
Almost every day
I do this all because I love you
Without a single dollars pay
During calving I'm the one
Who stays up to check cows all night
Sometimes just staying awake
Becomes quite a fight
I help you brand up all your calves
I also fix the meal that feeds your clan
I help sort to go to pasture
Which sometimes falls
Just short of disaster
I tear down your old fence
And help build the new
I also help fix the fixable
Which is becoming very few
It does not please me
When that cow gets by or
That fence isn't as tight
As you would like
Just remember when I'm out there

I'm trying real hard to give it my all
When I screw up I'm crying inside
I do my best and that's all I can do
So the rest of you can go get screwed
I'm sorry I'm just plain ole me
But this is the way I will always be

When my mom and stepdad moved to Florida, they bought a house with a good size piece of property on it. They were by a lake and had wooded area around them. They, like us lived at the end of the road. The back yard was beautiful with a pond and sun shelter and patio. There was an attached sun room and nice garage. They took both their dogs Lady and Shar with them when they moved. Lady and Shar were both beautiful Miniature Eskimos. I wasn't very happy about them moving so far away, it was hard enough seeing family as it was just going to Illinois once or twice a year if I could manage it. So I just knew I would never get to see them. They made good friends and dad got right back to working on his car projects and back to car shows and parades. Mom found herself a job to keep herself busy. It wasn't long before they had another kitty or two. They seem to be an attractant for strays. When dad wasn't working on cars he was helping out neighbors or doing his own projects adding on a deck to the front of the house and yard work. Mom would send me pictures of what dad would be working on this week or this month. He added a deck onto the front of the house and built a mantle for the fire place. He kept pretty busy. After a few years after moving to Florida Shar and Lady passed away, but it wasn't long before a couple scraggly dogs came wandering in from the woods. One they named Casey and he turned out to be a Vizla. The other was a Black Lab/

Staffordshire terrier mix who they named Cody. They placed ads in the papers and up at the veterinarians but no one claimed either one of them. So they had two new dogs. Mom and Dad came to Illinois a couple times and I was able to visit them and meet the new family members. They were big boys and so sweet. I kept telling mom I would try to come down to visit them in Florida. My chance came when a friend of mine wanted to go back to Florida which was her home state to visit. So we decided we would share expenses and carpool. We had a good trip both coming and going. She dropped a very nervous me at my moms and went on to her vacation destination. I'm not sure why I was so nervous but I was. Being away from home, sometimes I feel like a stranger around my own family, so that might have been the reason for the nervousness. I was there and lacked the support from my husband and my dog; it was just me, alone with my mom and dad. Soon after arriving I started to relax. I latched onto Cody and kept him as my support dog. He was such a big goof and so sweet. After my first night I began to relax and things went great. I really hated to leave when it was time because I had such a wonderful time. We went to several flea markets and rummage sales, then we played tourist at a few places, went to the beach and just had fun. Dad was building onto his pond so Cody could have a pond to play in. He decided Cody could have the old pond but the new one would be off limits. He built a bridge over the ponds where came together and I helped him place the liner in and we rocked it all up. Dad did a lot of landscaping around it. We finally let it fill up with water and it was a work of art only my Dad could do. While helping dad I couldn't help but notice his coughing. It was a sound I knew all too well from working at the hospital. We made a trip to the ER with dad while I was visiting. Dad was given some medications to help him with his coughing. I knew it was a temporary fix but didn't want to say it out loud because saying that word out loud would only make it real. Here I was with the dad I had wanted my whole childhood and I am losing him to cancer. I felt that was so unfair to us both. I was angry when I found out at fifteen my mom had remarried. I was too busy running away from my own problems and missed the wedding but when I got pregnant at 16 they were both there to help me through it. That's when I realized my mom was finally happy and I have not one dad but two wonderful dads. This dad, my stepfather, did all the things I enjoyed doing. We spent time going to rummage sales and auctions and flea markets. Mom and Dad had many cook outs and dinners at their place in Illinois and I enjoyed those times most of all. After my son was born he was flown to Peoria, Illinois to a hospital with a special unit for premature babies. Being a ward of the court I had to have a place to stay in Peoria in order to be with my son. My dad set this up with his uncle who had a three bedroom home and he lived there alone. That was good but not good enough for the state. I was not permitted to stay there alone with an adult male so mom and dad dropped their lives to stay in Peoria with me. They drove me to and from the hospital every day for several weeks till my baby could come home to yet another foster home with me. This home would be my last till I was able to get my own apartment. So when my mom called to tell me Dad had lung cancer, I wasn't surprised but hearing it out loud I didn't want to believe it. I cried for several days. I decided I needed to tell them thank you for the wonderful vacation I had with them. I sent that in the form of a poem. A couple months later mom called to let me know my dad was hospitalized. He was hospitalized at that time for a couple weeks. I sent him cards and letters and poems. He was in and out of the hospital several different times before he passed away. This was the hardest loss I had had. I still have bad days with this loss. I know I knew I couldn't feel the same hurt as my mom felt. I wished I was closer to home so we can be with each other during this big loss and in healing. My mom's sister, my aunt, lost her husband that same year. He and my dad were close like brothers. They spent many good times together at the lake homes they both had. They spent time fishing and doing things together. So it was fitting to have both their funeral services together. They were both laid to rest in the family cemetery. I wrote a poem for my uncle too. I read both the poems at the funeral. I am just glad Mom and Aunty have each other to help themselves through these losses. The following poems were a few I wrote telling my dad how much I wished I could take his pain away and how he wasn't just a step dad, he was my dad. I miss him so much. He was the life of a lot of parties.

Dear mom and Dear dad,
Thank you for the great time that I had
Thank you for all the food that was great
I should know I cleaned every plate
Thank you for all the flea markets we went
And for letting me spend all the money I spent
Thank you for all the new places we traveled
And all of the treasures we had unraveled
Thank you for all the enjoyment I got
Sorting all those buckets of rocks
I really enjoyed working with dad on the pond
That memory alone will forever be fond
Thank you for all the nice evenings we had
Just sitting out, on the front deck
Having you both all to myself
Really isn't that bad, what the heck
Thank you for being just who you are
And the wonderful time that we had by far
I'm just sorry it had to end
Because saying good-bye is just too sad
So beware to you both cause I'm coming back
So get my bed ready for the next Jamae attack

A Single Wish

I know you're not feeling well
Some days you even feel like hell
I wish I could be there to
take away your pain
I wish I could just wash this
all down the drain
I wish I could reach into
the bright skies above
And grab some energy
for you right from the sun
I wish that one special star
Would come falling from the skies
So I could make my wish
and give it to you as a surprise
IF only wishes could come true
I would make this wish just for you
right now I can only send you a hug
And tell you DAD that you are loved

My mom and step dad had these two little Miniature Eskimos. One was Shar the other Lady. Both dogs were rescues. Shar was the older of the two and a little shorter and more filled out. Lady was tall and slender. The grand children could never tell them apart; they were of course both long haired and white. Another difference was Shar was "the nipper" and Lady " the lover." When any of us kids would come over to visit, the grandchildren were immediately on Shar alert. I think at one point or another they have all had a nip in the butt from Shar. These two little dogs were treated like royalty. Both deserved the royal treatment, especially Lady. Her first home was not a pleasant home. She was kept in a small kennel in a dark room and her kennel was full of feces and urine. Mom and Dad saw an ad in the paper for a little Eskimo dog. They called and were given an address and upon arrival they had second thoughts, "they did already have one dog and two cats why do we need another dog"? Those thoughts that creep up on you and somehow you manage try to push them aside. We do have two cats, or will Shar get jealous, and would the two females really get along? You know those normal in the back of your mind types of questions? They both decided since they were already there what harm would it do to just look. The "just look" part is what got the best of the two of them. Dad decided they would not and could not leave that poor dog there in that dirty cramped kennel and then go home and try to sleep with that horrible vision in their heads. Mom was in full agreement. Now, little Lady, as she had already been named had found herself a new home. Her first visit was the veterinary hospital. She was in poor condition with hair loss, knots, and hot spots. Lady was given a haircut and medicine and then off to her new home. Both Lady and Shar found each other to be ok; they did the usual tail inspection and then it was tail wagging as if saying I am so glad to have you here. They enjoyed their walks together and playing by the pond and even taking a dip in it now and then. They really enjoyed chasing the bull frogs and barking at the geese and ducks. They did learn quickly when the geese get close to shore its best to get close to Mom or Dad. Those geese do bite hard. Lady and Shar became quick friends and even got along with those two spoiled cats. Each had their own beds and enjoyed company except Shar but only when the grandchildren came to visit. Mom and Dad never found out why Shar disliked children. Lady was the total opposite; she loved everybody. When Mom and Dad moved to Florida, the dogs moved also. I'm sure that was quite an adjustment for all. The dogs spent most of their time in the house where it was much cooler; the humidity just wasn't much tolerated after spending most of their lives in Illinois. Shar passed away five years after they moved. Shortly after losing Shar, Mom and Dad found out Lady had cancer. Two years later a tumor was found on her back leg and the doctor removed it. Lady struggled with the surgery and cancer. She was just unable to fully recover despite all Mom and Dad did to help her but the good Lord was looking out for both mom and dad. He knew what was about to happen so he sent Casey to them. Casey was a dog who was red in color that just showed up, skin and bones, one day while they were sitting out on the front deck. A trip was made to the veterinarian to see if he was micro chipped and to get him on the right path to healing. Casey was found to have no home and it was determined he was a Vizla Hound. Too soon the day came when Mom and Dad had the toughest decision to make and Lady had to be put to sleep. Mom called to let me know. It was sad and I struggled with the loss of Lady. I know it was hard for my parents to make that decision but that was what was best for Lady. I think my heart hurt most for my parents. For some reason when this call came about losing Lady it hurt more and my folks were hurt deeply. The loss of Lady was deepened by not having Shar either. Then one morning shortly after losing Lady, Mom and Dad were getting ready for the day and went outside to water the lawn and flowers. To their surprise, sitting at the front of the door patiently waiting for help was a big but very skinny and bloody dog. So watering was put on hold and the day's events would now be a trip to the veterinarian Dad decided this dog would be named Cody. Cody was now a new family member. He had a lot of healing to do thanks to the cruel person who shot him through the face. But it is strange how broken hearts can be mended with the saddest of events knowing you helped save the life of an innocent animal. Cody turned out to be a lovable black lab crossed with red nosed American bull terrier. I was happy to hear that Cody now had a new home and was going to heal from his wounds. After a couple weeks of Lady passing away a poem came to me about Lady so I began writing it down as it came in bits and pieces. When I was finished with it I sent it to my mom and dad. They printed it out onto a picture of Lady and framed it. So in doing so I guess they liked it. I have fond memories of both Shar and Lady. They brought my mom and dad a lot of love and enjoyment.

A Priceless Gal

She was our Lady
And quite the pal
She was a sweety
She was our gal
She didn't care for
Leather or lace
It didn't quite
Fit her pace
No running out
To various stores
To catch a sale
Oh! What a bore
She'd rather stay
At home with us
After all she was our gal
She never wanted
For diamonds or pearls
That wasn't her style
That was our girl
A fancy meal
Or a glass of wine
That would never do
For this Lady of mine
Her hair so perfect

With its shine and glow
A beauty shop
she'd never go
She had no use
For silver or gold
What good was it
If you still grew old
You see our Lady
Was a priceless gal
She was the four legged kind
Who make the best pals

After my stepdads and uncles services I had become very withdrawn. I had lost my step dad and three Uncles and my Grandpa had suffered a stroke. It was a very hard year. At work we had one particular person in upper management who seemed to make it their personal agenda to make my life hell. Things at work had become stressful to say the least. Several of us at work confided in each other and it was quite mutual: none of us enjoyed working here anymore. Some staff members who were classified "no rehires" had been rehired and that became a major stressor for me. This particular staff member was an abusive person, verbally and emotionally. He was fixated on me for reasons unknown. I made it clear to him I did not care for him; I was happily married and to leave me alone. I took these complaints to both the supervisor and higher upper management but it fell upon deaf ears. I felt lost and alone. I did everything I was supposed to do and I did it by the book. I became very depressed and grew deeper within myself. I tried to reach out to these professionals as to how I felt and how he was attacking me. The only advice I received was to deal with it and I had to work with him or find another place to work. So I tried very hard, every day going into work I would tell myself "you can do this, it is just one more day so be strong". When I was working on the ambulance I shuffled patient care to my partner when this guy was on duty in the E.R.

This was done to avoid having to speak to him or give him a report on the patient we would bring into the hospital; I just wanted to stay clear of him. Then out of the blue I was told I was suspended for 3 days: the reason being that none of the upper management would be at work and they felt I was walking up and down these halls angry and they believed I would blow up. That really pushed me over the edge. From day one I had done nothing wrong but was being punished. I was not an angry person; I was a person who had just lost her father and three uncles. I lived too far from home to help my grandma with my grandpa and could not attend two of the funerals; I had just recently attended my dads and my one uncles funerals. So I was still mourning over those losses. If not for these losses and suffering from depression and P.T.S.D, then YES, I would be a very angry and pissed off person but I was just hurting. I went home that afternoon and the more I thought about what I was just told the more I felt I was no longer wanted or needed. I was slipping away into a one way dark hole of hell. As I was pulling through our gate I just sat in my car and cried. I knew I had made up my mind and I didn't like what I was thinking, but I had to call my husband. I guess I hoped he would read my mind through the phone lines and talk me out of this; I just knew he would know what to do. I do not recall our phone conversation or much after that. I took a lethal dose of medication. At this point I guess he did not read my mind and so therefore could not save me from myself. I then drove up to our calving pasture about a half mile from home with my dogs following me. I do recall telling GOD how sorry I was and that I desperately missed my dad. I begged GODs forgiveness for this sin that I had just committed and was gone. Several hours later I found myself wet, muddy standing at my front door with Dalia at my side. It was as if I had been dropped out of the sky or put there and then I felt like I was hit in the chest to wake me up. I was dazed, confused and not in my right mind. I woke my husband up and as he put it, I was asking him why he "was in bed in the middle of the day." After asking this, he being an EMT, he knew my life was in serious trouble. I survived this ordeal due to the grace of GOD, my husband's quick thinking, my dog Dalia and our wonderful ER staff and flight crew. I am not sure how but I feel my dog was GODs angel to keep me safe while she guided me back home. Dalia never left my side, I easily could have been a meal for our resident mountain lion or have drowned in our creek. There is so much old equipment and vehicles around like many other ranches and farms. I could have ended up anywhere hurt or dead on this particular night. I decided GOD must have other plans for me or I would or should be dead. But for now I continue to work and write poems and I listen to my girls at work when they need an ear to bend. Someday I would like to talk to and help young girls get through their pain from their abuse. This particular poem is the result of that night.

These are my memories this is my nightmare
Weather you believe me or not
I WAS THERE I was there
Not a pretty place, no sunshine, nor even a flower
it's a cold dark damp dungeon
without light for no source of power
A candle flickers alone on a table
Providing little light with its small glow
Wanting to leave, I can't I'm unable
Frightened and cold the tears start to flow
I try the door one more time, please open
Back on the floor I sit in dismay
Still locked I found, I continue to sway
on this cold hard ground
Shaking from the dampness
I would pray and pray
Why am I here what does he want
I want to go home don't leave me alone
I'm locked in this hell unable to leave
The memories stay forever
it seems
everyday When your hurt
for a life time
You can never escape
Over and over you feel like your raped

Back in 1997 when I first met my husband I was going through a divorce and dealing with depression, and PTSD. Carl was the love I had needed in my life, not to mention my soul mate. Carl came to me at the right time in my life and with him came his wonderful family and friends. As I was introduced to his many friends, I realized what a nice group of people he runs around with. Several of these friends are his neighbors. For instance his good neighbors and second home the Walters clan. Frank and his brother Dave both lived and ranched on the same place for generations. Frank and Dave have always been there to lend a helping hand. They are both married to exceptionally wonderful women. Along with ranching, Frank was a teacher; his wife Evelyn shares that same passion and teaches too. Frank however taught in town at the local school and later taught in the country school where my son would end up attending after we moved out to the ranch. It was great having this relationship for my son. Frank became a good friend to my son at the time in his life he needed a neutral male influence. As Frank and Evelyn both decided to retire, life began to slow down for them. The ranch they kept for a few more years before deciding to let the cows go and lease the land as we have done. The work load is hard on a person's body and sometimes that outweighs the joys you get from the animals themselves. Giving up a lifetime of ranching is a sad part of life. You can almost say a person goes through withdrawal. You will still help out a neighbor from time to time just to be around the cows and calves, but eventually it has to be given up all together when your body starts to slow down and it doesn't cooperate any longer. Evelyn's mother Nora came to stay with them after her health made "life on her own" unmanageable. It soon came that after work a couple evenings a week I would stop at Franks and Evelyn's and I would assist Nora with her showers and getting her settled in for the evening. This did not feel like a job but an honor to be helping those who had helped me. The Walters clan never knew just how much they were helping me with the regaining of trust I was receiving from them but friendships go a long way to a person like me. To Nora everyone was family. She was everyone's mom or grandma. She was a most sweet and wonderful lady to have known. When Nora passed away it was a big loss to her family as well as to all who were blessed to have known her. She was a hardworking lady and still had time for her church and family. Her unconditional love was the reason I wrote this poem for her. Dave continued ranching and farming until his unexpected death in 2014. This was a hard blow to all who knew him. He will never be forgotten for his generosity and his infectious smile. I do hope someday I can come up with a poem for him.

For Nora

She watches the flowers as each morning they bloom;
She'll gently pick them
To brighten a room.

The sun she'll watch as it falls in the west.
It comes back the next morning
When the colors are best.

As spring rolls around, the baby calves come too;
Running' and jumping', lots of playing' they do.
She rolls with laughter at the sight she sees,
Watching those calves running through the trees.

She enjoys her grandchildren as they wrestle and play;
The laughter she hears
Brings memories to stay.

As she sits quietly
With the lights down dim,
She enjoys her memories of all of them.

Her thoughts then wander to a time way back when
It was first those two—
Just Nora and Ken.

As she lies so still, a smile crosses her face,
And she whispers so softly, I must leave your place,
For God is calling me, home once again
I shall be with my true love, my one and only Ken

Just before moving out to my husband's family ranch around 1998 I had bought my son a silver tip long haired German shepherd puppy. He had wanted his own dog for a while so I looked into some puppies I was told about by a neighbor. My neighbor and I took my son and together we went to look at these almost certainly cute puppies. As my son picked up each puppy he looked it over and cuddled it and would place it back down in the straw bed in the barn they were born in. After about a half hour of pure puppy loving he picked out a little female that he named Malachia. He just doted on this puppy day and night and he took care of all her needs. Malachia was about 4 months old when we moved out to the ranch and sadly enough just after about four months of moving out to the ranch both Malachia and Carls dog were poisoned. Someone had tossed some poisoned hot dogs onto the property and both dogs ate them. The local veterinarian at that time could not save either dog. This was quite a blow for us all, especially my son. I felt another dog would help, but was it safe? I looked to Carl for answers and Carl felt it should be safe. This was a first and it would be the last time anything would be so cruelly poisoned on his property. I wasn't looking for a puppy, but one had found me. On the way home from work one fall evening I found a puppy in the road ditch. Her litter mate had been hit and killed on the road so I worked hard at gaining her trust and coaxing her out of the culvert that ran under the road. Two candy bars later I had the puppy. My son fell in love with her right away and named her Kiah. He felt it would be nice to honor Malachia by giving this puppy part of her name. Kiah as it turned out was a Shepherd/Border Collie cross. She turned out to be a wonderful little dog. She was timid and fearful of vehicles, so we guessed she might have been tossed out of one or maybe fearful after witnessing her litter mate being killed by a car. She made up for that by turning out to be a wonderful cattle dog. Her only fault was she would not work cows for Carl. She would do anything with him except working cows. So I thought as a wedding gift I would get Carl his own cow dog. I found a good bloodline in the paper and called about prices and if they had any puppies left. The man on the other end of the phone line informed me that they did indeed have three puppies left, two black and white and one red and white and gave me the price. My heart sank when I heard the price but I really wanted to give him this gift. Since Carl is a red head I saved a red and white Australian Shephard/ Border Collie cross male pup for him. I really had no way of coming up with the money due to the upcoming wedding and I knew of only one person to call. I had never asked my dad for anything really my whole life so maybe he would help. This too was a big step for me and it would be even better if this gift came from my dad. I called my dad and explained this gift and the lack of money. After all, planning an upcoming wedding wasn't cheap. My dad sent the money and said to tell Carl it was a wedding gift from him. Carl loved his gift of the puppy and decided to name his new puppy and sidekick Buster.

Buster was a great dog; he took the place of three horse and riders when working and moving cattle. He was smarter than your average person. Buster knew his left and right and easy and actually any command he was given. He knew when we brought cows across the bridge where to put them, the same when bringing them down the hill. As soon as we would start out to different pastures he knew if we went left they would go four miles to this pasture and right would be a different pasture. He and Kiah were a great team. Kiah would always go with us during calving to tag calves and vaccinate. This dog had decided every calf had to get a lick on its nose by her. The moms weren't happy about this so a game would ensue. Kiah would always win and get her lick in. Buster and Kiah were always together, running up and down the creek and chasing rabbits. They were as close as two could get. Sadly after six years we lost Kiah to a human type form of Lupus. Buster donated blood to her and we were able to locate a few rare units of Oxygloben she so desperately needed and she was getting better until a secondary infection took her from us. It took Buster's heart a long time to heal; he took her loss quite hard. He quit eating, and it would take a force to get him to go outside. We decided to take him to the veterinarian. Our vet prescribed a medication to give Buster to help him get his appetite back and help with his depression. Our veterinarian is the most awesome DVM in this country as far as we are concerned and he is just a wonderful guy. We couldn't believe the changes we were witnessing as time went on. After about a year or so another puppy came to us, this one through an acquaintance at work. We adopted this little puppy who turned out to be a Catahoula. My husband decided to name her Sadie. She and Buster were great together. He didn't take to her right away; I guess he wanted to make sure she was staying awhile, but after a couple weeks she kind of grew on him. Buster had found his youth again and a new friend to run with. If you saw Sadie, well Buster was close behind. During calving season I always tried to take the night shift so my husband could get feeding and other chores and repairs done during the day. This also was a time I had to myself in the crisp cool night to reflect on my life and how I had grown not just as a wife but as a mom and a person who was now whole again. So every night when I would go out to check the cows Buster was always by my side. On this one particular night we had a freezing fog move in. It was a bitter night, one of those nights that you needed to be right there when the calf dropped or you would lose it. That bitter cold would freeze the baby calves little lungs. Needless to say that one night turned into a busy four days. Buster and I set out that first night into frozen fog and I ended up filling the cab of the pickup, floor included and some of the back, with cold calves. While I gathered up calves, Buster played tag with the upset moms. It just so happened we had a foot or more of snow before the fog, so that made it hard to run with a calf in your arms so Buster did the running while I loaded calves. I hated to tell Buster but he had to ride in the bed of the pickup; the babies needed the warmth and the seat filled up quickly as did the floor. I hurried to the house to get these babies inside by the wood stove and to come back up to most likely gather up another bunch. It seems like the cows are heaviest and just need to calve during the worst weather. Upon our arrival at the back door, we were met by a very large, upset, lost Canada goose! This goose was not a happy goose but one cold and upset goose. At any given time when the command of "Buster, hup hup" is given, Buster will get whatever is in your way out of your way or put it where you want it put. Well, that is except for tonight. Buster got out of the bed of the pickup and came running around to where I was standing to see what I wanted. He was met with the same greeting as I had been met with. One upset goose with its wings spread out and hissing ready to attack. Buster decide he would have no part of this goose that was blocking the doorway, but on the other hand he had to do something to save me so Buster ran to the side of the house to our bedroom window and commenced to barking. Eventually he managed to wake up Carl and he came to our rescue. Carl came with a broom in hand ready for battle; he did take a little bit of beating by the goose but Carl eventually got this uninvited guest to move over. By the end of Sunday night we had a total of 36 calves in the mud room, bathroom, and front entry way. We were ever so thankful that they had all survived that cold frozen fog. The hard part was getting moms to take their calves back. After a day or two we finally had all our babies back with their moms and nursing. The goose stuck around for a couple days so we fed and watered him. After the weather cleared up he returned to the skies and high tailed it to Florida I'm guessing. That's where I would of had gone. Out here on most ranches everyone has an old pickup or two that still runs and works fine to putt around the ranch with, or one they just can't seem to part with. We have a few of these pickups and one is an old 1966 Ford flatbed pickup that we use for caking cattle during the winter and early spring. This same pickup doubles as our fire truck during the late spring, summer and fall months. Buster's other job on the ranch was to keep the cows off of us during feed time. The cows would always come rushing the old Ford flatbed pickup to get to the cattle cake but by golly Buster made sure none of those cows came up onto his pickup. We did have a couple ole girls who would get their mouths right under the cake spout and let it pour inn. Good ole Buster even put a stop to that kind of behavior. He was determined these cows were going to be patient and straighten up while he was on duty. Buster would also keep the front of the tractor clear of cows when we would hay them. This made rolling out the big round bales or grinding the hay easier and it went a little bit quicker, by not having to slow down or constantly stop for a cow or calf. One day we decided it was time to test the bulls for reproduction purposes before turning them out with the cows. The bulls were kept in a small pasture east of the place about half a mile were our road ended. They had water all year round thanks to the creek that is fed by several natural springs and to our knowledge has never run dry. As we were gathering up the bulls for their trek up the road Buster was there to assist. The bulls behaved well until we started moving up the road. It never fails but this is when they decide it is time to fight one another. This was holding up the bulls that were not fighting and causing a stall out, out in the middle of the road. Buster got after them by barking but this didn't seem to faze them one bit. These bulls were full of energy having been out on fresh green grass and they know its spring time and when we show up to move; they know it's time to be with the cows. As a last resort we told Buster "come on get them, let's go, and move em, move em". So to him that meant tail time. Buster was the type of dog if they didn't move by him barking then he would latch onto their tail and that would get their attention and they would move. So that's just what he did! He latched onto one of the bulls by the tail and to Busters surprise he also got a mouth full of fresh green grass diarrhea. He stopped dead in his tracks trying his best to spit it out. I never saw a dog try so hard to spit, or spit at all for that matter; poor Buster. We got his mouth rinsed out and we started to move once again with the prize fighters. Buster went after the tail again for just a split second, he then remembered what had just happened and that changed his mind to nipping at the heels. Buster was never a heel nipper, but today he would be. Buster was a one of a kind dog. Life for the dogs were great for a few more years until we lost Buster in 2011 to an auto-immune system break down, and liver disease. Sadie went through the same mourning process as Buster had gone through when we lost Kiah. So once again we were off to our favorite veterinarian. This time the doctor had started magnetic therapy on dogs and cats. I would never of had believed such a thing would work but I would try anything for my four legged family members. Sadie had three sessions of therapy and with medication to entice her appetite our Sadie was almost back to her old self again. But Busters loss was hard on us all. We could only mourn his loss and give him a burial like the ones before him. After a few weeks had passed I was sitting on the couch in the front room thinking about Buster and all the wonderful memories he left us with. I felt the great dog that he was should get his own poem. He was my husband's right hand man. Not to mention the time or two he saved us both from harm and great bodily injuries. He was with us eleven wonderful years; he died at home with us by his side. All our pets are never forgotten. They hold a special place in our hearts. A poem for Buster on this day popped into my head, so I wrote it down. I'm not real pleased at how short of a poem it is. I wish a better one could had come to mind but it is what it is. It is short but to the point. Sadie however has never returned to 100%, but about a 95%. She is still to this day reserved. She is now afraid of gunshots and thunder and the smoke detectors short little beeps when they need a battery changed. She will go outside only on her terms and she is a bit moody. Buster, we are thinking, was her strength and together they were a force you didn't want to mess with. They, too, came home with battle wounds from raccoons and beaver and we can't forget the porcupines. But they always came home happy and smiling, sometimes wet and muddy and once or twice with that wonderful fragrance of an upset skunk, but always pleased with what they had accomplished. If they could speak the stories they could tell us would be a book in itself. All we can do is guess the story by the wounds. I was in Illinois for my families get together and was not looking for a dog but once again a puppy found me. Dalia has become my rock, so to speak. When I feel down or just not myself Dalia is always there smiling. Dalia has become the mascot for the Local Volunteer Fire Department. She loves to ride on the trucks in the parades and her most favorite time to ride is during home coming; that's when the football players are up on the trucks during the parade with her. Dalia played a big part in my recovery and in helping to save my life. Dalia is very special to me. She is always running around with her tail wagging and a big smile on her muzzle. The dogs love the freedom they have out here on this ranch and the wild life they can chase. We have no neighbors for two miles and the creek is their playground. They play in it all summer long. Whatever they do or injuries they get we know Doc will fix them right up. My husband and I, from the beginning decided no dogs out here would ever be left tied up to a chain. We tried the kennel once but the dogs climb out or dig under. So we gave that up. They have never gone far from home. When we come home from work the dogs are always at the door to greet us and out the door to see the world after our greetings. They are only a holler away when its meal time or time to come in for the night. When we have to be out of town for more than a day our pastor will come out here to stay with our animals and take care of their needs. Our pastor enjoys staying out to the ranch and he really likes the satellite TV. It is nice to have friends and neighbors like our pastor and his wife whom you can trust to stay and keep an eye out for your livelihood and four legged family members. They live 5 miles up the road from us and they run and pastor the church we go to. It's a small church but we enjoy it. On occasion when we are to be gone for the day and it is Sunday the girls Sadie and Dalia, and our wiener dog Tator are going with us for the outing, well, they too go to church. If it is too warm for them in the vehicle they will wait outside, unless an unsuspecting child would happen along and let them in church. They will quietly walk down the aisle in church, single file, I might add, until they find us, then they lie at our feet. So I guess you could say they go to our church also. We try to keep them outside but a few times a year they do go to church. They love to visit when we have the work groups in and during vacation bible school. The dogs and visitors both enjoy those times to see each other and to be fussed over. The same people come back yearly and bring a few new faces with them and they always ask about the girls. They are a big hit with everyone. It is nice to have a church who themselves have dogs and welcome ours too. We have on several occasions brought our horses up for the kids and adults to ride. Most of the groups that come during the summer months are from big cities and have not ridden a horse or even been close to one. This is a big treat for them. And we have had a few come down to the ranch and we've taken them out riding around the hills and spent a day just enjoying the horses and scenery. It is beautiful country out here in GODS country. Life is good out here for us all. Riding horses out here in the big open spaces up and down the hills is very therapeutic. It is quiet with so much wild life to catch a glimpse of and maybe snap a picture or two of. It is awesome to look out your window to see deer or elk in your yard and eagles flying in the sky above your trees. There is so much to see and take in. My favorite time to ride is in the spring time when I'm out riding down through the draws and across the hills; you can smell the vanilla smells coming from the pine sap. It is the best smell, and then you have all the wild flowers and alfalfa blossoms. It is all beautiful. It's no wonder I have such happy dogs. The cats are pretty happy critters also. They find plenty of things to catch and chase too. We have four geese that are happiest when they are chasing the cats and dogs. Dalia however thinks it's a pretty intense game when they chase her. She plays along and smiles with her tail wagging. Sadie however doesn't have time for such games or a thing to do with those crazy geese, and just as well keeps her distance. We will catch one from time to time just to hold them and let them know we are not going to hurt them. Why these geese feel the need to be so darned mean is beyond me. After all I raised them up from babies and need them to keep the rattlesnakes out of the yard, and this job they have done quite well. They are perfect for this job because they are very territorial, too. They have their swimming pool and a hydrant we water them from. Anyone who crosses this imaginary line around that area is fair game to them, horses included. We had some of the neighbor's horses wander down the road on a few occasions and they wandered through the gate to come into the yard. We were outside at the time and actually got to witness our fearsome geese run this herd of about twelve horses back out the gate. This was such a funny scene to see. It was a shame we didn't have our camera with us. I try to keep a camera on me quite a bit when I am outside or riding around on horseback or checking fence while riding the 4-wheeler. I have found a love for taking pictures and out here there is so much to take pictures of. The dogs go and follow me everywhere; they love to ride on the 4-wheeler with me or get off and run beside me. Tator will even ride on the horse with me.

We have prairie dogs and that becomes a big issue with our hay field and crops. They completely destroy acres of land and the holes cause major injuries to livestock. When a horse breaks a leg from hitting a hole the horse has to be put down due to they really can't be fixed. With that said I will take the dogs up the hill to chase prairie dogs; they seldom ever catch any but they have a great time trying. After running around they will go swimming in the big stock tank. The big dogs tire out way before little ole Tator does, he just keeps on a chasing. One day little Tator got lucky and caught his first and only prairie dog; poor little guy was just as surprised as we were. The prairie dog was a big one and managed to wiggled out of Tator's grip and was just jumping at his face biting at little Tator. As the prairie dog jumped up towards his face Tator would jump back as though he wasn't sure just what he should do. Well, Dalia knew and she came out of nowhere like lightning as she flew under the barbed wire and saved Tators life (I'm sure Dalia thought). They were all tired out after that day of fun. Back down to the house we went and they played in the creek before turning in for the night. I just know Tator dreamed about his mighty big catch and Dalia she dreamed of saving Tator from the crushing jaws of that wild animal. Many a times our dogs saved one another. One instance happened to be Buster and Sadie saving the life of another little dog we had. I was walking down the road one late afternoon enjoying the fresh air and exercise when our little dog wandered over to the road ditch to potty on a tree. I am just guessing the inhabitants of this particular tree didn't see this as one bit amusing because in a flash I had five raccoons on top of my little dog. I was shocked and scared and hollered for the two big dogs and I found a stick at the same time. Like a flash the big dogs hit the pile of raccoons full force and I had my stick trying to get everyone sorted out. Just as quick as this battle had started it had ended and the raccoons had dispersed. I just knew my little guy was dead but there he stood just looking around wondering just what in the world had just happened. This little dog did not have one mark on him; the other two had some scratches but nothing bad and I was so grateful and to this day I am not sure why that happened and why this little dog survived without a mark on him. I miss old Buster to this very day and this poem is for him.

Buster

A good cow dog is a ranchers dream
A good cow dog comes few and far between
A good cow dog knows his left from his right
A good cow dog knows just when to use his bite
A good cow dog knows where the herd should go
A good cow dog will even work in the cold deep snow
A good cow dog will keep his people
and herd from harm
A good cow dog will even tolerate
others who live on the farm
A good cow dog will work in the summer's heat
A good cow dog doesn't care if
your appearance isn't neat
A good cow dog has your back when
there's a fence to mend
A good cow dog is a rancher's best friend
A good cow dog will always be in need
A good cow dog was our Buster dog indeed

After my attempted suicide I was at home for a couple of weeks. I had a lot of time on my hands and didn't care to do anything. I spent most of this time crying and talking to my dogs. I started to notice how Dalia would not leave my side. I knew from the day I got her as a small puppy that there was something special about her and it finally hit me. This dog knows I am hurting. She really knows I need help and she is telling me she is here to help me. I thought to myself how ironic that this dog knows I need help but humans did not. I spent many hours talking to Dalia and talking to my therapist about Dalia. Dalia always accompanies me to my sessions and attends them with me. Sometimes I feel like those who have never gone through trauma or abuses don't understand how we feel. It's like that saying "those who live in glass houses shouldn't throw stones." I wish every day I live, I could live without the knowledge of what I have gone through. I told my husband after coming home from work during a break down that I didn't ask to be molested or raped, I don't want to be that person but I am. Those are hard words to say and even harder to live with. Being a mother and grandmother I pray every day my grandchildren never have to live life the way I do. I am so different on the inside and I know that now. It has taken so many years to see that. I don't look different I am just more cautious and aware of all my surroundings. I have also learned that some wounds are so deep it takes these much longer to come to the surface so the healing can begin. I couldn't walk into a gas station to pay for gas if it meant I was alone in there with a man. I would wait till several people would go in and these people had to be other women or families. I still to this day don't trust being alone with males. I may never feel comfortable around males. It doesn't make any difference if they are family members or not. Having Dalia with me helps with the comfort and keeps me calm but that lingering thought of rape never goes away. I am glad that I am finally starting to get to the point that I am no longer afraid to talk about what I have gone through. I have always felt it was supposed to be hidden away and never spoken about, but I now know in order to heal you have to want to heal and keeping all your hurt or anger inside just doesn't work. Writing has always been a good outlet for me. Others who have gone through these similar abuses find painting or sewing as good outlets. I know there is an outlet for everyone other than dying. Those two weeks at home were the longest and hardest two weeks of my life, so I thought. All I could think about was how I wanted to be at work. I love this job and I missed my girls there. I just prayed I could come back and everything will be better. I know my life will never be the perfect life like others have that have never had trauma or abuse in them, but I am very lucky to have the husband I have and the girls I have that I work with. I am most thankful for the Lord who gave me a second chance to see how lucky and loved I really am. During my stay at home my mom called several times. She was never told of what I had done and it was unusual for her to call me out of the blue like this. We would visit and before hanging up she would always ask if I was ok. I lied and said yes. Somehow she knew to keep calling till I finally broke down and told her "no, no mom I'm not ok." And through the tears I told her everything. I am so lucky to have a mom who even at 800 miles away could tell something wasn't right with her little girl. I work in a facility full of professionals, three of whom I begged for help from and yet did not receive help of any kind. But my mom knew, she felt it in her heart that I needed help. A week after telling my mom what I had done and all I have been going through I received a beautiful necklace in the mail. My mom sent me an angel. I know I have many angels in heaven already; I know my grandparents, my stepfather and GOD are watching out for me. Here on earth I have my wonderful husband and an awesome but goofy dog named Dalia watching out for me. I am lucky to have a mom who just knows and doesn't give up when she knows I need her most. It has been almost four years now since that day and I am still in therapy and I am still fighting to be permitted to have Dalia, my now service dog here at work with me. For some of us the battle never ends. I have been asked to speak to some teenagers at a summer camp about my experiences and how I see things in a different light from others, due to my abuse. I have accepted this challenge. I think it would be good to share my story in person, with this age group of teens. Dalia will be right by my side to help. She will love every minute of it. Dalia is a lover to all children and adults alike and this will be a great adventure for her. And another adventure and step for me. I hope this will lead to me speaking and helping youths at risk in different places. I really wanted to thank my mom for not giving up until she was told the truth and for the angel necklace. I sent her this poem I wrote. I love you mom. To know my family and having nine brothers would help you to find the humor in the ending of this poem.

MOTHERS KNOW

A mother knows when your heart is shattered
A mother knows when you're emotionally battered
A mother knows when you're world is falling apart
A mother knows by the beating of your heart
A mother knows when you feel there is no hope in sight
A mother knows how to make your world right
A mother knows when you are beaten down
A mother knows, just how to fix your frown
A mother knows when you are too weak to fight
A mother knows how to help you see the light
A mother knows when your heart needs help to mend
A mother knows, because she is your first best friend
A mother knows for her love, is a love that will never end

Thank You

"thank you" comes in many shapes and sizes
Some may come with great big surprises
Some thank yous come from across the miles
While others may come with just a smile
Some may come with a laugh or a giggle
Others as a card that folds in the middle
You have those that come with flowers in a vase
While others come with a puppy to chase
Some could be as sweet as kitten to cuddle
Or a bit damp from a mud puddle
However you're thank you has come a bit late
But now you will no longer have to wait
Your thank you doesn't come with a story that's told
Nor does it come with a picture to hold
Your THANK YOU comes straight from the heart
with a big I LOVE YOU ooops I have to fart

In April of 2013 I lost my grandpa to a stroke and heart attack. He and my grandma are the world to me. They played a big part in the person I am today. It would have been so easy for me to have turned down the wrong road in life. Their love and understanding and faith in the Lord and introducing us kids to that same faith has helped me to choose this better road. We spent most holidays at their home when we were children. We are a big family and I am their first granddaughter. I like to think that makes me a tiny bit special but we are all treated equal. We attended Sunday school and church during our childhood years. Mom and Grandma were both Sunday school teachers, so we felt we were even more special. Every Sunday after church Grandpa and Grandma would take turns taking each grandchild out to lunch so they could spend special one on one time with us. I have 5 brothers: the twins are Randy and Robert, then there's Jacob, myself, Matthew and Paul. When my dad remarried I gained three stepbrothers, who I have known my whole life: Donald, Charles and Kenny. I also have six cousins; only two of them are girls. The three of us granddaughters would get together and stay weekends at Grandma and Grandpa's house. We would play with our Barbie dolls on the big bed in my grandparent's bedroom and watch with pride as Grandma would get ready for work in her nursing uniform. Back then they dressed in all white with their white nurses hats on their heads. She always looked beautiful. Grandpa always gave her a kiss on the cheek as she would leave, with us still blushing from witnessing this little bit of affection between our grandparents. As children we would always ask Grandpa to tell us the story of how my dad lost his finger when he was a child. Grandpa would tell us Dad and Uncle Tom were working on the mini bike downstairs and Thomas jumped on it to try it out before Dad could get his hand out of the chain and it took the finger right off. Grandpa took the gloved finger and buried it out in the back yard. Grandpa never told a single person where he buried that gloved finger and has taken that secret with him to his grave. These are just a couple of my fondest memories. My grandparents did a lot of traveling throughout the years and always had a camper. The different campers Grandpa would buy throughout the years were his pride and joy. He enjoyed sitting out there piddling around with them and was more than eager to give anyone a tour of them. When Grandma and Grandpa would come home from their many adventures they always brought us kids back a gift. I most of all enjoyed the photos they took. I still look at those pictures especially the old black and white photos of Great Grandparents and family members. Whenever I go back home to Illinois I enjoy going through them with my children and grandchildren and telling them the stories my grandparents told me about each picture. Whenever I go back I always call some family members and we will go out to Bob Evans to eat. It usually ends up being with my dad and stepmother "Judy" and grandparents. No matter the time of day Grandpa and I always ordered biscuits and gravy. This is and always will be our favorite. We would go back to Grandma's and play card games and just have a good visit. We still get together at Bob Evens but the biscuits and gravy will never be the same without Grandpa to share them with. Grandma has now moved to an assisted living complex and enjoys visiting with her friends, most of who live in the same complex. The complex is next door to Grandma's church so she doesn't have to drive across town anymore to attend. I have nothing but wonderful memories of my Grandfather. He was a quiet man but he was also a good man; he helped to build several houses that are still standing today back home. He was a city employee and also worked for the parks and recreation department and I remember as a child we would go to Miller Park and watch the fireworks on the 4th of July. I would tell everyone I saw that evening, that it was my Grandpa across the lake setting off the fireworks. I would just beam with pride. When I was told of my Grandpa's passing I was just numb. I guess it was disbelief or I never thought this day would ever happen. These things happen to other people's grandparents, not mine. I thought I would try to write something for my Grandfather and surprise every one by reading it at his funeral. I did just that and I also surprised myself. I was very nervous but sitting in the front row next to where I was sitting was my Grandmother. I looked down at her beautiful face and read my poem after saying a few words about my grandfather. I did this not just to prove to myself I could, I also did it for her. My Grandma is my shining light. My Grandpa will always be special to me and missed every day. I will see him again when its time, this I know for sure. I love my Grandparents mainly because they had done so much more for all their family than they could ever imagine. They did this out of love and everything they did or said came straight from the heart. I know when I lose my Grandmother it will be a very hard time for me and I will need a lot of strength to get through it. I may or may not have my service dog Dalia but I pray I have another just like her. I will be surrounded by family but my true family is and has passed away in many forms, such as my pets. They are who I am closest to and tell all my secrets to without being judged. I pray my mom is still around as well as my dad and stepmother, and my true love, my husband, but if not, it will be rough waters once again. I just need to continue my trust in GOD, my husband and my service dog.

Grandpas are Forever

Everywhere you look- you see a bit of Grandpa
In every little corner-and every little nook
Outside in the flower beds, where his once strong hands
Worked up the soil
Right here in the carport-
where he spilled that drop of oil
downstairs we see his ole tool box
amongst his special pile
his tools laid out carefully
unused for quite a awhile
with every child within his family
we see him in their eyes
some have his laugh others his smile
some of us his wisdom as we just sit
and think of him awhile
for others that memory may be
his favorite hymn in a book
Grandpas friends may have a special
memory of Grandpa at work
we all have a little part of Grandpa
whether it's just a memory or his looks
or just enjoying his pictures in the photo book
laughing at a joke he once told
one thing is for certain, Grandpa is in our hearts to hold
I KNOW
Cause Grandpas are forever, just look around you and
remember

I vaguely remember when my Grandma H. moved to California. I know she moved out there when my Aunt moved and it was after Grandma had sold her house. I don't remember a lot about that particular time in my life. I was going through my own problems and running from my feelings. I was hiding a lot of my feelings from my family. I remember my mom telling me Grandma's house had been sold. That was somewhat of a surprise to me since I had no idea it was for sale or even why Grandma had left it. After the house was sold I started having dreams about it. The times I spent with Momma Kitty and always stuck playing at that park. I never have quite understood the dreams but figured it was Just a normal reaction to missing home and never getting to see the old house and walk around inside it one last time. I spent a lot of evenings baby sitting inside this house and I never got to say good-bye. Mom's side of the family would get together at Grandma's to visit or have a good family dinner. I was never close to my cousins on my mom's side of the family because they were all about fifteen years or so older than me. The one cousin who was my age lives in Oregon and I think always has. Whenever we would go to Grandma's the adults would visit and my brothers and I would always walk up the block to the park. I know the park became a very scary place to be and I would whine around about how I hated the park. But I would go and watch the others having fun. The park has this big tall old cement block water tower, which still sits there today. We would play around there and pretend an old giant lived there. I think at one point we actually believed one really did reside there. We always wanted to go inside but were never able to. It was always padlocked. When we would get tired of playing at that park we would skip on over to the school playground and play there; it was only a block away. That was just one block behind my Grandma's house. When we would get done playing we would go back to Grandma's and we would rest under the old pear tree that sat out in front of her house. So at the right time of the year we could eat fresh pears. My favorite part about going to Grandma's was she had Mama Kitty. This cat was the only cat Grandma had while we were growing up. She was just a regular gray striped tabby cat that wandered in as a tiny kitten. I spent a lot of time on Grandma's back porch talking and petting that old cat. Back then there really wasn't a lot of spaying and neutering going on so every year Mama Kitty had a litter or two of kittens. I would love holding and playing with the kittens and then when they were old enough Grandma found homes for them. About three years ago my mom called to tell me the man who bought Grandma's house was going to tear it down and rebuild. That is when the dreams came back and more frequent, just about every night. It was always about me and my husband going to Illinois to clean Grandma's house out because the family left everything in it. All those memories and I had to save them. I was losing sleep over these dreams and never understood why it meant so much to me. Then a couple years ago when I went home to visit, there stood the new house. I was so saddened to see the old place gone. After seeing this new house where my Grandma's house used to be helped me to have some sort of closure. Just as suddenly as those dreams appeared they too were gone. But a poem for some reason emerged from all this.

Grandma's House

Grandma's house keeps calling me
It's in my thoughts and in my dreams
The house now emptied
Family and friends no more
Old and worn are its wooden floors
This creaking house with its tiny halls
Now has bowing and emptied walls
Its windows cracked no longer clean
The doors on their hinges forever lean
This house once full where family embarked
While us children played at the park
Out in its yard sits the ole pear tree
Once provided shade for my family and me
Grandma's house is lonely and sad
It only wants back the family it had
Grandma's house keeps calling me
To save it from a strangers dream

Through the years working here at this facility you get to know a wide variety of people. We have had many staff come and go. I have been here through so many different upper management personnel and have come to realize no two are alike. This is true about supervisors as well. My first supervisor in the department I worked in was great. She was easy to get along with and really cared about this facility. I worked with her for five years before she decided she needed a new beginning. Her children were both living out East and she wanted to try to get on with a facility out there. When she decided to move she put in her notice. I was really nervous about my job. I wasn't sure how this would end up or who was taking her place. I threw her a big going away luncheon party. We had a great time with friends and employees with years of stories to share. She was very special to me; we saw each other through good and bad times. She is doing great now and has two grandchildren she loves to spoil. I wrote her a poem as a thank you for all she had done for me. After Bethany had left I continued to work and did my best to make this place a good place to work at. I then went full time in the office. My new supervisor, I was glad to know, was Cathy, who had been working in a different area. Ever since she started working at our facility we had become well acquainted with each other. I have found my dogs were good at helping me open up to talking with other people within the work area. Cathy was a pet person same as I. So it was great having her on board. I learn from my mistakes and some mistakes I have to make more than once. This was one more mistake I hope I will never make again. I allowed myself to open my heart up to her before really getting to know her well. I figure if she was a pet person she must be a good hearted person. Well, this is not always so. Some people show you the side of them they want you to see and like. But then there is that other side; the true person they really are. I thought I was doing great but little by little, piece by piece I was being torn apart by two people who I thought I could trust. My walls were starting to be built back up around my heart and the monster of depression was working his way back in. I knew I was going downhill but like an avalanche I didn't and couldn't stop it from happening. I felt as though I was on the outside of my body watching myself slowly die from the inside out, but I could not help myself. My request were simple, all I needed was to have my service dog be with me at work. I needed her more now than ever. I was slowly slipping and couldn't pick myself up. I tried to explain to myself why? Why did I let this happen? Why did I let my guard down? All the whys in the world could not help me now. I will simply have to help myself, so I will gather my strength up and call on GOD and we will get through this tough time once again together. As for Bethany, she is doing well and is the happiest she has been in years. Needless to say I sent her off with a poem.

Dearest Bethany

There's a lot to say
As our tears well
We will miss you so
We would love you to stay
Your job was not easy
As some of us know
You put your best foot forward
As you helped this place grow
You weren't just a supervisor
But became quite a friend
You were tough when you had to be
And still helped many hearts mend
We've watched many staff come
And even more staff go
But none of them near
As dedicated as you
We all now know
This job was your life
For the past fourty two years
There were many accomplishments
Frustrations and tears
You saw it all through with

Love, determination and
The phone to your ear
You will be greatly missed
by all of us here

During my time working at this facility I became really close to several of our residents. I knew and still know many of our residents, but working closely with them day to day you get to know them to be more like family. I would always take one of my two dogs to work with me. It was a treat for all. The residents would just perk right up and my dogs loved all the attention. The dogs are Sadie, she is a Catahoula dog and Dalia my service dog who is a Dalmatian mix. They both love coming to visit and are loved by most staff and residents alike. I would bring a ball or a tug toy for them to play with and the residents loved watching them run up and down the halls chasing the ball. This was good exercise for both. We had one little lady who had suffered a stroke during her stay with us. She no longer could speak and didn't recognize her own family members any more. After her stroke she went to rehab and was out of the facility for several weeks. After returning to our facility I brought Dalia to work with me. One of the residents reached out to Dalia and called her Sadie by accident. Well that didn't set well with our little lady who had had the stroke. For the first time in over three months she spoke! She told the resident that this was not Sadie but in fact her name was Dalia and at that moment she reached out to Dalia and started petting her. All our jaws just dropped; for months she had not spoken a word nor would she even move her arms and here she was doing both. And she did this all without any assistance. I was so proud of my dog and this resident for what I had just witnessed. All Dalia noticed was a lot of hugs from this resident and she ate it right up.

Another resident I was quite fond of was Mr. Straus. He was the number one ball thrower for my girls. Mr. Straus, like most of our residents was wheel chair bound, and an American Indian. This fact of being wheel chair bound never slowed him down one bit. Mr. Straus was quick at maneuvering his chair; he could out run most of the staff. He would be in front of you one moment and down at the end of the hall the next. One day I was doing paper work at the office and Mr. Straus was next to me just visiting and a tiny little lady approached, (she was a new resident) and she asked me if he, pointing at Mr. Straus, was a chief. I looked at Mr. Straus and asked him, "Well, Mr. Straus, are you a chief?" This brought a big smile to his face and Mr. Straus giggled a bit and replied shaking his head up and down and said, "Yeah, I'm a chief." So I told the resident, "Yes, he is Chief Wheels Real Fast." Mr. Straus just laughed and the little lady just as serious as she could be answer, "I thought so: he looks like a chief." After that Mr. Straus told everyone with a giggle he was Chief Wheels Real Fast. When we lost Mr. Straus, a few of us at work took it upon ourselves to do flowers and fix a meal and serve it to his family during his wake. To all of us Mr. Straus was our Grandpa; he was the most lovable and funniest guy anyone would have the pleasure of knowing. We get a few residents like this from time to time. Those are the ones who make us feel like we do matter and we are proud to be allowed to work for these residents and care for them. I wrote a poem about Mr. Straus and had it printed on a picture of him and Dalia playing ball. I had it framed and left it for his family. Mr. Straus will always have a special place in my heart.

Chief Wheels Real Fast

Mr. Straus you are the man
You were the boss
We miss you so much
We miss you Mr. Straus
We miss your smile,
Your laughter, your love
We miss your each and every hug
The dogs too will miss you Mr. Straus
They enjoyed chasing
The balls you would toss
We loved how you would laugh
As they ran up and down these halls
They always brought you back
Each and every ball
You both enjoyed playing this crazy game
How they will miss you
Your loss is such a shame
You brought so much laughter
We all had so much fun
That light has now dimmed
You were our shining sun
We will miss you so much
We love you Mr. Straus
You are the one
You were the boss

When I started working at this facility I was part time in two different departments. I enjoyed my job but was yearning for something more challenging. So I took some classes and after getting my license I transferred into another department. There I worked with one of the other girls and we became pretty good friends. She had been working for the facility around twenty yrs. Her oldest son worked at the facility too, in housekeeping. This young man and my youngest son knew each other well and talked about opening up a tattoo parlor together. But that would never come to be. In April of 2008 this young man became a victim of suicide. With this tragedy we lost an awesome and talented young man and a good employee. After this horrible and sudden loss his mother would go on to help to get a Suicide Prevention Project up and running and also works on suicide prevention and awareness on her own. Every year she holds a suicide awareness walk and dinner. We pray for those who we know that have passed on and pray we won't have to bury anymore young people to suicide. I have recently learned that one of the larger reservations has declared a suicide state of emergency. Tribal leaders said suicide was the number one leading cause of death among teens. I was shocked at this finding. Suicide has become an epidemic amongst our military heroes coming home from war, too. There has to be more awareness for this and help for these young people who feel this is the only answer to their pain. We need services to help these military families and our soldiers coming home from war and suffering from PTSD. We now have higher rates amongst our first responders, EMT's and paramedics from all over the United States. Suicide cannot continue to be the answer, not in this day and age. It is such a sad and high statistic, one that should not have ever gotten to this high rate.

One day at work I was approached by my co-worker and she asked if I could write a poem about her son for her to display at the conference that she would be attending to represent The Suicide Prevention Project. I told her I would try but I couldn't promise her anything because I can't just sit and write poems, they have to come to me. It took a while but I finally had some words scratched out on paper and started writing. When I was finished I took it to my co worker and she was pleased with it. We printed the poem off with a picture of an eagle soaring over the clouds. I know this young man would have appreciated this poem. We still lose a lot of young people and more soldiers and emergency personnel to suicide all over these states of ours. The youngest child to take their own life out here was only eleven years old to date. As I write this page I realize our community just lost two young girls a little over a week apart to suicide; one was twelve the other fourteen. I wish I knew how to stop this epidemic. We are taking one step at a time with putting awareness out there in our community and trying to bring as many younger children on these walks as we can. This is just one step in the many we will be taking. But until we get more help and more facilities to help these children and soldiers and emergency personnel, I'm afraid we will lose many more than we care to count.

Our Sparkling Star

Our Dearest child our oldest son
you were that bright sparkle
in your mothers eye
that sparkle now dim
since God has taken you
still we ask and wonder why
we now see you
in the darkened sky of night
you are that beautiful star
that shines so bright
you are that eagle
that we see soaring
gracefully through the hills
watching closely as
your loved ones try to heal
you are that wolf who sits proudly
high upon that grassy knoll
guarding over his family
as they play safely below
you are the wind that gently
brushes over your mothers face
reminding her to dry those tears
and save them for
a joyous place
you are that one warm spot
in your mothers heart
there she holds you

night and day
there you will always stay
you see son you never
really went away
you are always with us
watching and guiding
your Loved ones
in your own special way
so every time we see
that eagle soaring or
feel the wind when it
will gently blow
we will look above and take
a moment just to say hello

For as long as I can remember my Grandma and Grandpa have always had a dog. The first dog I remember them having was Candy. Candy was originally my Uncle Danny's dog. I remember the day my Uncle Danny came home to announce he had found himself an apartment and wanted to show Grandma and Grandpa. He was so excited that he had found himself this apartment; this would be his first home he would have and this also meant a bit of freedom, too. Grandma, Danny and I, and I think Grandpa, too, all went to look at Danny's apartment. It was a nice little one bedroom; I still remember the color of the counters and part of the layout. He had bought himself a puppy and named her Candy and was starting life on his own. My Uncle Danny was the greatest; he was the youngest of Grandma and Grandpa's boys. They had no girls. He was fun to play with and always had pennies all over his bedroom floor; I'm not sure if he was messy or tossed them on the floor for our benefit. When any of us kids came to visit Grandma and Grandpa he would let us clean them up. Uncle Danny worked for the city and was on the road crew. One morning while at work he and a co-worker were working on a man hole and as they were both climbing out of the man hole a drunk driver had ran through two separate barricades and collided with my uncle and his co-worker. The co-worker passed away on scene and my uncle passed away at the hospital. I was about seven years old when we lost Danny. My Uncle Danny was the world to me and I have always missed him and think about him often. I always wondered what he would be like. Would he have found his true love and gotten married? Would he have had any children? These will always be some of the many unanswered questions I will never have an answer to. When I was 18, I was with my aunt in the grocery store picking up a few items for supper. As we came around to the cooler section she pulled me aside and asked me, "If I tell you something do you promise not to cause a scene and say nothing to this man?" I was a bit confused but I nodded my head and replied that I would comply with her wishes. As she nodded towards this man in the beer section she continued to advise me that this man who was filling his cart up with beer was the man who had hit and killed my uncle. My aunt had to hold me back from possibly hurting this guy. I was so angry! He took this great man away from our family and here he was buying beer. Had he not learned anything from this? Like my Grandma says, "He will someday answer to GOD". But he doesn't and never will know the pain he caused my grandparents and so many others. And let's not forget to mention this little dog that my grandparents were left with to raise and so lovingly held dear and close to their hearts up until the day little Candy passed away. When that day came they were deeply hurt by losing their only link left of my uncle they held so tight to. This little dog did not know how much she helped them with their grieving. No, this man obviously will never know. After Candy passed away it was a couple years before Grandma decided she had really missed having a little dog around to hold and love and to care for. When Grandma finally decided to get another little dog she found a little Mini Pin that she named Amber. I don't know why I never wrote poems about either Candy or Amber. I figure none came to me till this last little dog Tony. After Amber's passing Grandpa was the one who was grieving and needed the companionship more than Grandma did. Grandpa was in a slump and I think he was depressed; growing older is so much harder on the man of the family than it is on the woman. At his age he needed a reason now to just get outside and walk. When they had Amber he was always outside walking her and now he wouldn't even get out of bed to eat some days. So Grandma decided another dog was needed to help Grandpa to find some purpose to keep going on in life. Grandma went to her local veterinary clinic and let them know they were looking for a small dog once again to fulfill their lives. After only a week or two Grandma received the phone call that she had been praying for. A woman who was moving out of town and was unable to take her therapy dog along was looking for a home for him. The lady had explained Tony was used at her former employment to help residents with their depression and loneliness and where she will be working next she would no longer need Tony due to this facility having their own live in pets and she just couldn't bear to leave Tony at home all day locked in a kennel. Grandma did not even need to think about taking Tony home; she knew he was their new family member. Tony was a Jack Russell/Chihuahua cross. He was the sweetest and calmest little dog. He was full grown and house broke and the bonus for Grandpa's needs was Tony being a therapy dog. Grandma's main goal was to get a dog that would help with getting Grandpa outside to get some exercise and also to be a lap dog for her to love. As it turned out Tony became more Grandpa's dog than Grandma's, but Grandma accepted that. Tony came to her for food and water and to go out to potty, but after that he was on Grandpa's lap or outside getting his walks. Grandma felt Tony knew who needed him most. They enjoyed Tony for several years. Tony passed away less than a year after my Grandpa had passed away. It seems as though when Grandma needed Tony he was there for her needs and in her time of grief, but as soon as she was doing better he felt his job on earth had been completed and then allowed himself to pass away. These two losses so close together were especially hard for Grandma. She felt she might of had done something to lose Tony or did not do enough. I told her with C.H.F. in a small dog there was nothing more that she or her vet could do than what she had done. Tony was pampered and well known to the veterinarians; Grandma took him for regular checkups and just to see that he was ok. Grandma, in some ways, was like a new first time mother with her newborn baby. Tony was with her much longer than expected. I think Tony held on as long as he had to, to see Grandma through her loss of Grandpa. His last year on Earth Tony was Grandma's lap dog. Grandma would always tell me that Tony never quit looking for Grandpa and he would lie in Grandpa's empty chair whenever Grandma was up and doing household things but when she would sit down he always found her lap. I felt I needed to do something personal for my Grandma since I could not be there in person when she lost Tony. I sent her a card with this poem inside.

The Empty Chair

Grandma went to the vets, for a visit to pay
A pet they wanted, to fill up their day
The phone call she received in just a short time
A dog they could have, if decided he's fine
Once meeting "Tony" they agreed he'd be great
A dog given up to a good home they would make
Tony was a special dog, well behaved, no trouble I recall
Much comfort to Grandpa I'd say most of all
Tony stuck to Grandpa just like glue
In Grandpas chair they sat, just those two
When Grandpa became ill and had to go
Tony became upset, he just didn't know

He searched all around from room to room
He was so sad and laid around with such gloom
Tony was lost with Grandpa now gone
Their chair now empty no lap to lie upon
Tony knew Grandma was grieving indeed
For both their comfort, his affection he'd concede
With Grandma much stronger and fresh blooming clover
Tony knew it was his time to cross on over
In heaven with Grandpa together again
Tony is healthy and happy to be with his best friend
I LOVE YOU Grandma,

Being an EMT we see a lot of children who are living with abuse, hunger and have a very unstable home life. It's not just in our community, it's all over. This is a sad truth. We have children who are brought into our ER's who are physically and sometimes sexually abused. These are just some of the worst cases I see. It brings sadness and memories flooding back to me. As a professional you have to push aside all your feelings and only focus on your patient and what is in front of you. Most of what we see is alcohol and drug fueled actions. There is so much of this in our community and not enough money for programs or jails to keep these abusers off our streets. Most importantly we need stiffer laws. Most of these abusers are on government assistance programs and don't work or contribute in any way to society. When these people get their government checks and food cards they sell the cards for cash or they trade for alcohol and drugs. The working class pays for this through taxes. As working class citizens when we apply for jobs we have to agree to regular drug testing to keep our jobs while the abusers get paid and keep on abusing. The children come out on the short end by going hungry or living off what are easily accessible-chips, candy, or uncooked Raman noodles. These programs were set up to help the children. Where's their help now? With the statutes of limitations, most all of us who have been abused will never see justice. Those who set these laws are the same people who sit behind their desks and turn a blind eye to what the real world sees and lives through every day. Children, and even some adults, fear for their lives and for the lives of family members when they are being abused. Their abusers make these threats real and you believe whatever they tell you. It takes years, if ever, before you feel safe enough to come forward and tell a trusting person about your abuse. By then it's too late to get justice and see that abuser behind bars. The government needs to cut off these abusers assistance and start drug testing those who receive government assistance. Someday, maybe the law will be changed for the younger generations and the younger generations will get their justice. The rest of us will keep looking over our shoulders. It will be a day of celebration when our blind law makers will open their eyes and hearts to see the world for what it really is. It took years for me to tell anyone about my abuse. I finally told my case worker the day I was emancipated. She promised I would get justice. Well that was a big letdown. But by this point in the game it wasn't my first. The hardest disappointment to hear and live through came about when I was 15 years old. I was a ward of the state and was placed in a state facility. This facility was a co-ed home. I pretty much kept to myself and earned points towards getting free time outside the grounds to go to the store or to just walk around. I was abducted by a man in a red convertible car. He pulled off to the side of the road asking for directions. I leaned in to ask what he needed and of course he grabbed me by my arm and the next thing I knew I had a knife to my throat. I was ordered to get in. He drove to a drive through liquor store; it resembles the little coffee huts you see around today. I was ordered to keep my head down while there; he picked up his beer and he drove on. I was ordered to drink while he drove us to his home. It was a nice, newer two story home in a cul-de-sac. I was scared but knew if I stayed calm and didn't anger him I might make it out alive. He raped me in his living room on his family's sofa and did what he wanted to me and after he was done he sent me to the restroom to clean up. I knew I had to somehow save evidence. I took off my sock, used it to wipe myself up with and put the sock back on. During this time I ran the water so he thought I was cleaning up. I was then dumped out on a county highway. A truck driver came along and gave me a ride to get help. Help I never received. What I got were two officers who claim I was just one of those whores from Cantrell Hall and got what I was asking for. I thought I did everything right. I gave them his semen on my socks and all the details that I could remember about his height, race, about the house, the car, even the liquor store. I have never been so ashamed, angry and disappointed as I was that day. I told them he was a family man. He had a wife and a child I saw them in a picture. I never received justice that day or any other day. I knew then and there I would never speak of this again. If the law won't help, then who would? I decided I would just be alone in this battle. When I went into therapy this last time, this was when I talked about the rape. It was hard to talk about and my family still doesn't know. I will someday find the courage to tell them. I hope the officers who are on duty these days are a bit more compassionate than these two men were. I hope this rapist wasn't a serial rapist who could have been caught in 1980. I pray and often wonder if I was his only victim. After leaving the co-ed home I lived in a variety of foster homes until I had my first son. I was then allowed to get my own apartment and take night courses to graduate. Oh yes, graduation, this was another let down. I was pregnant and all I wanted was to attend high school and enjoy what life I could. I was told by the principal, who just happened to be my Jr. High principal and had transferred to high school, that he had the pleasure of letting me know I would not be allowed to attend since I was pregnant. The reason being was I would make a bad impression on all the good girls. The only bad thing I knew I had done was I chose life over abortion. When my son was eight months old I met a very nice and wonderful man named Mike. He was thirteen years older than I was but he was good to me. When I mentioned I would love to take night classes it was Mike who helped me with the classes by watching my son and driving me back and forth. Without Mike's help I could not have done this on my own. I took my GED and passed just to be told there had been a mistake since I could not graduate before my class graduates. So I had to wait and retake my GED two years later when my class graduated. Mike taught me I was worth something and I was stronger than I thought I was. He taught me how to drive a stick shift and an automatic car and how to ride a motorcycle. He helped me buy my first motorcycle which was a little 125 Harley Davidson, I love this bike and I still have it today and will keep until I die. Mike and I were together for five fun filled and wonderful years before going our separate ways. Mike is still a great friend to me and all of my family.

Writing this book has brought a lot of bad memories to the surface but has also helped to remind me I had good memories hiding in the back of my mind too. Now I can continue to move forward and live with all that life has for me to experience. I have survived a lot of heartbreak, abuse, and disappointments in my life. The biggest disappointments came from the very people who were placed in positions to help young people who are victims and need help; all I received was rejection. I look around me daily and know some of the girls I work with are survivors too. They live in silence and suffer alone. The area I live and work in are full of these types of victims; many of them don't know who to trust or who they can talk with. It isn't just out here; this is an epidemic in most of our states. Most of those who are victims and who do know where to go to receive help can't get a ride to get this help; they live miles away from safe houses or have no phones. It's hard to leave a spouse or the father of your children. I have come to realize out here if you turn in someone for abuse of any kind you will suffer retribution from their family and extended family members. It is never just cut and dry out here. This is why suicide is easier for a lot of people. For some of the younger kids, rape and or abuse is a daily part of life. Telling a parent may make it worse. For these kids, the parent might be so strung out on drugs they don't care. For others, using the child is how they obtain their drugs. Some of our younger people are also turned into caretakers for their elders. These kids only want to be a child and go to school but are forced by their parents or family to take care of and bathe and wipe after toileting their charge. They are forced to stay up day and night to care for their elder and when they do get to school they are too tired to stay awake. For these children life is over before it even begins; in their minds there is no help for them either. We need to help our children so they can help themselves. We need social workers who truly care and listen. We need these workers to be fresh and not burned out. I feel my social worker was burned out and never really listened. I am sure many children feel that same way. We need to get more of our high school kids interested in this field of work and give them incentives to go to college. We should make college more accessible for those who can't afford it. The sad truth is there will always be a need for social workers but will we have enough social workers for the need? I wrote a couple poems from what I witnessed in life and saw in other children I have worked with out here.

SORROW and PAIN

How does one start a poem
full of sorrow and shame
When ones heart is so full of pain
How does one receive forgiveness?
When so many out there are to blame
How do you ask for forgiveness?
Without exposing all their names
Who can one trust in this world that we live
When those who are to blame
Are those who we cannot forgive
With all the evil that waits out there
We not only fear the dark of night
We also fear the day of light
No longer are we safe in our yards to play
For evil lurks around the corner
Just a moment's notice away
LORD help us fight these evil beast
For our children are who they choose to feast
If we don't many lives will change
It only takes a single day
Can I ever learn to forgive?
So I can have the life I deserve to live

Only Seven

GOD is that you?
You know I'm only seven
so can you tell me
why I'm in heaven
did I do something wrong
mommy always yells at me
when I try to sing you a song
I try hard to behave
I keep my little sister quiet
We hide in our special cave
Why is mommy and daddy so mean
Sometimes I wish this was all just a dream
You know how I got all these bruises
I tell them I'm sorry
When I make them mad
But they still hit me
That's why I'm so sad
Look God my bruises
They are going away
Now I look pretty for you today
GOD how is my little sister
Will you bring her here too
Without me at home
She won't know what to do

Can I go see those other kids
Maybe they will let me play
But GOD we can talk later today
Oh one more thing GOD
Can you tell me when my sister is here
You know she might be very full of fear
I'll need to hold her hand today
Then we can teach her how to play

Glorious Place

Dear grandma,
What's it like in heaven?
Is it really bright
With the warm sunlight
Dear grandpa,
What's it like in heaven?
Are the streets really lined with flakes of gold
Is heaven really a special place
where nobody grows old
Dear mommy,
What do you like about heaven?
Is it all the pretty flowers
that grow all year long
Or is it the bright blue skies
With the big beautiful butterflies
Dear daddy,
Tell me all about heaven,
Do you like the all day fishing
Are the lakes clear blue and really pretty
I bet you have a favorite spot
Where your fishing line will never knot

Dear GOD,
I'm in heaven now
As I'm sure you know
And it's just as beautiful
As my family had told
there are no children hungry and crying
how great is this to see
that you had kept
my pets for me
Thank you lord for allowing me in
This is such a wonderful place
theres no abuse and its free of sin

My husband has always told me you can do anything if you just try. You are a smart woman. This advice was a shock to me. For a large part of my adult life I was told just the opposite. This statement took a while to sink in. I kept repeating what Carl had said to me over and over again in my head. Is this true? Am I smart enough to do anything I want? Am I too old to even try or learn new skills? I decided I would at least give him the benefit of the doubt and try. Carl has always encouraged me to apply for a job at the hospital. This first step was hard but I did put in my application at the hospital. To my surprise I was hired. This was a magical moment for me. To anyone else it would just be a job but for me it was a big step which was a hard step to take and it would mean a lifetime of achievements to come. I really enjoy my job there. After a year or two at this job my husband asked me to partake in the EVOC class. This class is the Emergency Vehicle Operators Course. I was very hesitant about that. My supervisor Bethany and I talked about it and even went out to the ambulance garage and sat in the ambulance checked out all the switches, lights and sirens and then we both decided it would be fun to try. So we took the course together which made this a bit less scary I guess you could say. We made it fun for ourselves as well as for the instructors. I found myself coming out of a hard shell I had built up around me for years. My first few trips as an EVOC driver were very scary but Carl made sure he was with me until I felt comfortable enough to make these ambulance runs on my own. The hardest part is backing into the ambulance stalls at the ER's. My first solo trip I did hit the wall a little, but come to find out I wasn't the only one to do this. I'm just glad we have good bumpers. My worst trip was taking out the other hospitals light and our ambulance light but I haven't hit a wall or light since. Backing those big ambulances into what appears to be small stalls does take practice, but a person does catch on eventually. It has been a lot of fun and a great experience. After a couple of years as an EVOC driver Carl was putting together an EMT class. He once again approached me to take this class. Carl has been an EMT since 1992. Carl loves being an EMT and had advanced to becoming an AEMT and also excepted the ambulance directors position, so I knew it would mean a lot to him for me to become an EMT also. This actually terrified me to the point I was pretty much ill during the first class and to say the least could not pass the computer testing. I had it in my mind I would fail, so I did. I retook the course and was more comfortable the second time around and passed both the practical's part again and the CBT's. Being an EMT has really made a difference in my life. I now feel I can help this community by helping its people when they are in need. This job and this book have really helped me to heal myself. We work side by side with our local fire department, as well as our local law enforcement. We get a wide variety of calls with a large area to cover. We see a large variety of injuries, accidents, and abuse. If we need an extra hand or two, our firefighters and officers are right there to lend it. We have each other's backs, so to speak. Law enforcement are great to have with us; they will show up most times before we call them or at a moment's notice if we feel a certain address or scene could turn dangerous for us. This feeling of safety is important to us as well as for our patient. This type of work is at times emotionally draining but a GOD send too. We see things no person should ever have to see. Until you are in this line of work you think these kinds of injuries or abuse are only in the movies; people don't really do these things to other people. All the beatings and stabbings, the sexual abuse, I understood to be real, having been down that road myself. But to see with my own eyes this happening to so many others was hard. It is real and now I am caring for the abused, and sometimes the abuser, but it is part of the job. You don't always like it but it is still part of the job and as a professional every patient is treated equally. You can't pick your patients but you can pick the right choice to give them the best care to your ability. This is why GOD saved me so I can help him save others. ONLY GOD can be the judge and jury; that is not our job. Most days are good and rewarding. The mutual working relationship and bonds we form with the fire department is most rewarding. They are the reason for the next poems I have written.

A Volunteers Night

The sky was so dark
The night too calm
I was lying in bed
Thinking of the day to come
Suddenly a bright flash jolted
From the darkened sky
Like a sword piercing the clouds
As they floated on by
With the sound of a crash
I was jolted from my bed
I ran to the window
With a heavy heart of dread
Then out of the dark
A monster arose
With fingers so fine
As they burned in my nose
I scrambled to the floor
As I tried to get away
The monster was behind me
Light headed-I began to sway
I coughed and I sputtered
As I was gasping for air
Its hands were so tight
I cried out in despair

The pager rang out
There's a house that's on fire
It's clear out in the country
This could take quite awhile
To the fire hall we gathered
Our warm beds left behind
These are our neighbors
Would flash through our minds
The second page rang
It has spread to the barn
This pierced through our ears
With great sense of alarm
The chief hollered "All trucks would now be in need"
As we all scattered
with grace at high speed
We arrived on scene shortly at hand
As the neighbors watched
This monsters grand stand
Our friends stood watching
With disbelief and horror
As this monster blew off
Their now blackened front door
A scream belted out "The children are in there
They just have to be saved"

As the fire men ran towards the house
For this monster to brave
The ambulance crew sat closely near by
While the firefighters fought back those flames so high
Through the eerie black smoke
The fire fighters appeared
In their arms were those children
Now ashened and scared
Their body's so limp and oxygen deprived
They were brought to the ambulance
Thank GOD those children survived
With the barn still being tackled
The animals had been freed
Thanks to our firefighters
Who are quick on their feet
All went pretty well on that frightful night
Just the interior of those buildings
Were lost in this fight
With gratitude to our firefighters
And ambulance crews
For their quick response
While the coffee still brews

An Angel Appears

I woke up hearing my mommy screaming
My daddy was yelling
I had never heard this before
Was I just dreaming?
I think it was smoke I was smelling
It was so dark, I was so scared
I ran to my closet,
to hide from my fear
I heard so much Crashing
And that's when I knew
The monster had made
His way through
I crawled deeper into my closet
Here I would just wait
In hopes someone would come
IF they didn't get ate
I need to know, I've got to see
Was he close enough to get me?
I saw his sharp and jagged teeth
Ripping and tearing at my door
I could feel his hot breath
As I lay frightened
on my closet floor
I remembered what mom

had always told
If ever you are sad or scared
No matter young or old
Pray to GOD you're never alone
That's just what I did
I prayed and I prayed
I told GOD what mommy had said
You send angels down to help us
They come in many shapes and forms
GOD- I sure could use an angel now
Just then I heard a big crash
It came through my door
In that moment my angel appeared
It was so cool-
He was decked out in fireman's gear

When visiting my family this past summer a funny thing happened. My son Jacob and his girlfriend Hailey joined my husband and me. We had a good trip back home, we dropped them off at my oldest son's house and Carl and I went on to my mom's house. It was a long trip since we drove straight through. My mom was in bed I am guessing because it was only 2am. Mom had given me the code to get in the front door but for some reason it would not work. I would punch it in, turn the knob, push the door and nothing. After the third time of trying I was surprised it worked when I fell into the house. Oh, this time it opened! As I was falling I hollered, "Don't shoot, Mom, it's only us!" Well, you just never know. My dad was all about safety and security. So when Mom lost dad and moved back to home she kept that in mind. She had my brothers put in a security system as soon as she moved into her new house. After falling into Mom's house and waking her, Mom got up and we visited for a little bit. The next morning I woke up knowing I was home at my mom's, because the smells coming from the kitchen wake you up. Mom always cooks big meals when we are there. My mom loves to cook and misses cooking since she is alone now, so it's nice to visit and cook with her and do dishes together and visit while doing so. I miss being around my mom. I wish I would have spent more time at home learning from my mom and bonding instead of running around as a teenager. Now that I am older I understand how important these special moments can be in one's life. You can never get these times back. It always appears as though when I am home I am constantly on the move. I think to myself this is exhausting, bouncing from family member to family member. I don't always get to see everybody but I sure do try. During our trip we would visit Grandma and, oh yes, we have to go to Bob Evens and eat with Dad and Judy. I would take time to do my rummage sales on the way to and from visits. I always find one or two things a grandchild or church member could use. Jacob and Hailey came out to Mom's for an evening and we all played cards and had a good time and did so much visiting and sharing memories and stories. I remembered one thing Jacob mentioned in one of our visits. He was upset by how people would look at him and his brother as though they were criminals or drug users only because they have tattoos on their arms. This made me feel really sad; I wondered if my own extended family members had treated them in this manner. I pray they did not but something happened because my own son will not go back home for any more family reunions. And he will not talk about it either. I hope he will someday change his mind. During our visits mom always tells us to place our dirty clothes in the basket on the washer. My mom must miss washing clothes, too; she always has to wash them for us. We learned there was no arguing with her about it, and Moms always win. So we abide and she kept us in clean clothes and the last night there she made sure we had only clean clothes to take home with us. After getting home from our trip I was unpacking my clothes and putting them away when I noticed a bra that didn't look like mine. You have to understand my mom got all the boobs in the family; my cousins and I were left with very little. I called my mom to let her know one of her bras had escaped and came home with me but not to worry, I would send it right back home. But I couldn't send it home alone so I wrote a poem to go with it. Mom got a laugh out of this one. And Jacob; I felt should have a poem too. He deserved this recognition and I pray if you read this maybe you will not be so quick to judge a person on their looks alone.

Lackin

Our boobs weren't made for floppin
But that's just what they'll do
Without you're bra you're boobs
Are gonna flop down to your shoes
When you are out there walkin
The neighbors will start watchin
Because your big ole boobs
are out there just a
flippin and a floppin
I just can't let that to happen
So your bra I'll just send back
It doesn't fit me anyways
That's the one place I do lack

Office Tools

He stands so tall
his tools he uses,
not to fight or cause abuses.
To down a tree or remove its limbs,
that break so often
in the wind.
His looks are rugged
with his tattooed arms,
but a heart of gold
that beats like ours.
He builds the lines
to stop the fires
that threaten the homes of
those who look down
upon the less desired
They are the ones
who see him shopping,
to buy the groceries
he takes while chopping
They see him in line and
think only the worst
not knowing his hand
is the hand
they should shake first
Tall trees he climbs
way up so high
one might think

he could wipe a tear
from GODS eye
The trees he removes
that are buggy or dead
burn the best for these fires
to get ahead
He is out there working
no matter the weather
to keep your homes safe
and your lives much better
as the sweat from his forehead
continues to drip
the heat from the sun
dries out his already chapped lips
all the while you're safe
in your homes of high tech
this young man has vowed
to always protect
he is out there a cutting
while the bitter wind whips
working hard at stacking and burning
for a trail to build quick
all the while you look
down on him still
His suit an old T-shirt
his loafers are boots
his slacks are old blue jeans
his office now burnt
His tools are not light
but heavy Stihl saws
he keeps them well sharpened

to cut through it all
He may not always look clean or
smell fresh of a shower
but he is still quite the gentle man
who works long-hard hours
This man that I speak of
comes few and far between
he is tall and well built
yet muscled and lean
I love this young man
and hug him dirty or clean
I am proud to call him my son
Jacob Robert Lee

The Golden Cup

Tall and slender and quite the man
With a heart filled with love
He works towards his plan
He works real hard
Pouring hot molten Steele
Working long hot hard hours
And that's for real
When not at work
To school he must go
To earn that degree
Before the doors close
A better life for his family
Is what he is after
At times he misses out
On hearing his children's laughter
This young man's life
Has always been hard
But giving up has never
Been in his deck of cards
He pulls himself together
And moves right along
With GOD by his side
He continues to stay strong
He coaches football in winter
And baseball all summer
Coaching these children
is never a bummer

with dance recitals and cheer practice too
not to mention school plays
and clinic waiting rooms
he gets very little sleep
but knows he can't give up
because a better future
is his golden cup
this young man I write about
is too my pride and joy
I could never be more proud
Is my first baby boy

My Grandpa and Grandma H. were always a joy to visit as a child. It was a special treat to be with them because it didn't happen very often. I remember as a child visiting them. I would always get to go shopping for dresses and girly things. They felt little girls should look like little girls and so it was. I enjoyed this special attention because my brothers weren't around to take this from me. I was for at least one day and night a princess. I miss those days when I was with them and made to feel special and loved like nobody else. I don't recall when my grandparents moved to Florida but I know my grandpa was around for both my children when they were born. I always took pictures of my grandpa holding my boys and one I especially like because I see the love for this baby in his face. My grandma was special to me too. I always admired her for how she looked and how there was never a flaw in her appearance. She too like my other grandparents was a GODLY woman and she and grandpa were very much involved in their church. She was always so beautiful and her hair and makeup were perfect. She was my grandpa's true love. I always wished I could have spent more time with them both but miles and work kept us apart. I did spend a week with my grandpa when he was in the hospital; it was one of those bitter sweet types of visits. "Grandpa is dying of cancer," was the answer my mom gave me to my question over the phone. Why and how could this be? These were only two of the questions I had for GOD. He went to church and was dedicated to GOD and he was a good man. I just knew I had to go see him just one last time, but how. I talked it over with Carl and he booked me a plane ticket to home and gave me his credit card; talk about true love. Mom and dad picked me up from the airport and at first light we hit the road. I rode with my mom and stepdad and my brother Robert to Florida. It was a long drive, and yes, we drove straight through to spend as much time as we could with Grandpa and Grandma. We had good visits and we all spent one on one time with him. It was hard to leave when we had to go back home but it was for the best. Grandpa said he was only hanging on to see his favorite granddaughter and to tell me he loved me. He was also holding on to see his children. Quite a few of us made it to see him before he passed away. I miss him so much but I know we will all be together again someday. I was hoping to make a trip to see Grandma, too, before she passed away but I wasn't quick enough. I was told she would not have known me and she didn't look herself. I am glad I have her in my mind the way she always looked. This is how I prefer to remember her looking. I always wondered why we all seem to find time and money for funerals but we can't manage to get together to spend more time as a family while we are still here on earth. I do know I am not wealthy and sometimes I have to get a loan from the bank to make the funerals that are out of state. If I were wealthy I would see all my family most every weekend. I feel very strong about family time. I love my family and wish we were living closer together. I really hate missing all the sports my nephews are achieving in and my grandchildren's games and cheerleading and dance recitals. But we all know as life would have it we must go where the jobs are and for me where my heart took me, and had me stay. When I go home I enjoy my family and visits but they are tainted by memories I can't get out of my head. I know I could never be happy living there. I am happy here with Carl and my dogs, horses, kitties and my geese. I now have two lovely and sweet donkeys. They are a joy to have as part of our family. My Grandpa and Grandma and I talked about this when I did go to Florida to see Grandpa. They both agreed I do look happier than I have ever had looked and they are happy for me. I don't know why but I did have a poem come to mind for my Grandma. I guess that means I will be reading it at her services and those same little butterflies will once again flutter in my stomach. I hope everyone enjoys it. I know I wanted to see her one last time but I couldn't. But we will all be together someday, I am sure of this. I love and miss you both, Grandpa and Grandma.

Grieving

Losing a loved one is always hard for me
So when I lose a loved one
The future is much harder to see
I know Grandma is now in heaven
So we should all be happy
Instead of crying and grieving
Let's all cheer up and dry our tears
think of the good times we have had
with her throughout the years
I always admired Grandmas beauty and class
It was great how she never put up with
Any ones no nonsense sass
Grandma was always so sweet
As a little girl spending time with her
Without the boys was such a treat
Grandma is with Grandpa in heaven now
all we have left are memories and photos
and our lives will continue on somehow
Losing a loved one is always hard for me
Knowing they are in heaven with GOD
Makes that loss so much easier you see
That's how I seem to get through life these days
Knowing my loved ones will be there waiting
when GOD leads me down his golden pathway
losing a loved one is always hard for me

A Letter from Heaven

Please my family don't cry for me
I'm in heaven with the Lord as you can see
So dry those tears, put a smile on your face
I'm with your Grandpa, and Philip
In this most joyous place
So please my family
Take that ache from your heart
And fill it with happiness
For our brand new start
We haven't left you completely alone
You have our life time of memories
And the many photos we have shown
So please my family
Don't be angry or sad
For GOD let us stay much longer
Than he could have
So please my family
Be happy for your grandpa and I
We are together with the Lord
So try not to cry and
wipe that tear from your eye

As a little girl I had always had a love for horses. My brothers and I always had to walk to school. So like most children we would of course goof off along the way. Sometimes we would play in Sugar Creek or I would cross the road where there were boarding stables. Just about every day a couple horses would be grazing in the paddock awaiting some attention. I always wanted a horse and was determined to own my own horse someday. My friend Brandi was a horse lover too. When she got her pony she spent most of her time with him. He was boarded at these same stables so we stopped there on our way to and from school to take care of him. When Brandi grew up she started up her own horse training and boarding stables and is now in charge of a college equestrian program. She is doing what she always dreamed of and I am so happy for her. When I bought my first house it came with several acres of land. I felt my boys could grow up here, have horses and join 4-H. I bought a couple older horses to start with and a year later bought a very spirited Arabian, Midnight who is the grandson of a famous Arabian in the California area. Midnight, however, has taught us all how to be cowboys. He was a show horse and trotter, also known as a harness race horse. He was 5 years old when I purchased him and throughout his life he was always taught not to break trot. So we had a challenge on our hands. We were all bucked off on a regular basis trying to teach him to be a saddle horse. After about two years Midnight finally decided it was ok to run and run he did. He turned out to be the best cow horse you could ask for; he was quick to turn and could stop on a dime. He would never tire and he never let a cow or calf get by him. He was quick and sharp. The boys joined 4-H and had fun doing the horse shows and trial races. As they grew older they went on to football and basketball but we kept the horses and we still enjoy riding. I still have that Arabian; he is quite the old man but has never lost his spirit. I have since bought a few others who are younger; one is a very tall and big registered paint. I don't understand how he is considered a Paint since he only has a quarter size white spot on a coat of red, located on his left shoulder. I also have Belle who is a registered quarter horse. She is a beautiful chestnut mare who also needs to be broke, so I work with her when I have time. Captain, the big red paint, is broke but just needs to be ridden more. Since we have retired Midnight my husband and I don't go riding together any more, since we have only one broke horse, so Captain doesn't get ridden often enough. Captain is the type of horse you only want experienced riders riding. I stand about 5' 2" and his shoulders are taller than my head. We have never measured him in hands but some day we should. He is hard to halter and saddle up but once done he does ok but spooks easily. So when a person rides him they better pay attention or they will find themselves sitting on the ground. I have broke several horses and sold them and I am breaking a couple now whom I will keep. They are both Appaloosas. One is a half blanket black Appaloosa and the other a full blanket red Appaloosa. The black I named Moon Shadow and the red I named Starr Dancer. They are very sweet boys. I bought them straight out of a pasture and neither had ever had human contact until I received them. They were a very young 4 and 6 months old when I got them. Along with the boys came a gray Appaloosa mare. After getting her halter broke and broke to lead I had to have her spayed due to my boys were still studs and our neighbors up the road have several studs. I named this mare Morning Star. I decided to start working with her right away since she was already two years old. She was gentle and a little more trusting than the boys, and just a great horse. I had her taking a saddle after our first year together. It was slow working with her to gain trust and I also have my other job to go to, so I worked with her when I could. Since hunting season was coming up and the gun shots spooked her I decided to turn all the horses out until spring. There was no point working with her until then, so I her out with the rest of the herd. Between the house and the far north-east fence there is about three hundred acres for them to run in. We had a pony and a couple extra horses being boarded at the place too, so Morning Star was happy to be with the rest of the gang. To my surprise, my son Jacob came down to the house after hunting one day to inform me of a dead horse laying on the other side of the fence up north. I went up to check and to my shock it was Morning Starr. Our resident mountain lion had gotten her. We are thinking it was most likely going after our pony or Midnight but when the horses get to being chased Morning Star will jump a fence. While jumping this fence she hit ice and slipped and we think that's when the lion got her. Before we could get a tractor up to retrieve her for burial the lion had drug her off. I was so hurt by this loss. I always dreamed of having a gray Appaloosa and here I had the perfect one and now she is gone. This spring I brought the two studs into the corral to work with them. It took about four months of working to gain their trust and get halters on them; now it was time to learn how to lead. With some grain in hand and patience, I got the job done. Once that part was accomplished it was time to have them castrated. I am currently working with them to get them broke to ride. I do it slow and gentle because at my age all things are done at a very slow pace. I believe in building their trust not breaking their spirits. I learned this through my life as having had my spirit and trust broken. Both are very sweet and coming right along. The morning I had their surgery done I hauled them to our veterinarian to drop them off and I went on to see my therapist. Going to my therapist is a weekly visit for me. Afterwards I brought the horses on into town to work with me. This gave them more time to heal in the stock trailer before taking them back home across our gravel road. Before coming home we had a class to attend so I drove over to where the class was taking place. The woman whom I bought these horses from the two years previous is also our class instructor, so she was able to see the big change in them and how much they had grown. I felt like a proud momma with these two boys. They had such slick shiny coats and had grown up quite a bit. They are quite shy with strangers but with me they are more than friendly. Moon Shadow is the more serious of the two and Starr Dancer is a bit of a clown. It's amazing how they have such different and unique personalities.

They have never offered to try to kick me but Starr Dancer did try to play the biting game twice but a couple slaps on the muzzle has stopped that bad behavior. While waiting for class to begin I started day dreaming and this next poem came to mind. This poem is pretty much what I get to experience several times a week. It is a great feeling to have in my life. When my horses come down our hill to get grain you do feel those hooves shake the ground under your feet and they stop just inches from your body. I close my eyes and it is awesome to feel their breath on my face and to smell their fur. I love my life and I love my horses.

AS THEY WEEP

Why GOD won't you let us pass in our sleep
When we hurt so much, we only weep
Why do you force our hand at play
It's no game to die this way
We don't want to tie this noose
We only want the pain to let loose
We would prefer to not go this way
But GOD you have forced our hand at play
Let's grab the bullets
Let's load this gun
Shall we pull the trigger
Just for fun
We are tired of repeating ourselves every day
We have now ran out of words to say
Let's take a pill
A red or blue
I have to laugh
Because that won't do
We need a handful of good opiates
And chase them down with a quart or two
This is how our hand will play
When we run out of words to say
If GOD would let us pass in our sleep
It would be so much easier
For our families to weep

Every year I have come to learn there are two separate
buffalo round ups that take place in South Dakota. I have
always told myself "next year you will attend and take part
in the round up." I still plan on doing this but getting my
horse broke is a challenge. The horse I had planned to use
this year was killed by our resident mountain lion. Now
I have to start over with a different horse. I am hoping to
attend next year's round up. The round I plan on going to
is "the big one" which takes place in Custer State Park and
has now become a whole weekend long event with chuck
wagons, music and fun. This "big" event I am told brings
in thousands of spectators from all over the country.
Friends of ours have attended this event every year for
several years. It takes a quick, and alert, rider and horse.
If you have a slow old horse with a non seasoned rider
you may as well stay home because you are only putting
yourself and your horse at risk along with whoever has
to rescue you, if a bull or cow with calf decides you are a
threat. Buffalo are considered a wild animal and like any
wild animal will attack if it, or it's young are threatened.
We are in their territory chasing after them, so this will go
one of two ways, one being they will go the direction you
want them to go or they will take flight and move you out
of their way. Luckily you will have those few heads that
have made this journey a few times so know this routine.
Having ranched raising cattle I am quite familiar with

stubborn cattle who prefer to stay put and whom are very protective of their young. Cattle and buffalo alike have no problem taking out after a horse and rider. Some people look at a big ole bull or buffalo and think they are just a slow dumb animal who they can outrun. Buffalo can run up to 35mph and when that head goes down and they paw at the dirt, well this means "it is on" and you best get to running and hope your horse is fresh and fast. Just being out there with these majestic beasts is quite a treat in itself that most people will never get to experience. I am lucky that I live in a state where we are quite familiar with buffalo and see the often up close and know their traits. This round up is a great opportunity that I have decided I will not pass up. I have several horses to choose from now so I just need to get them up to par and worked. I would love to show my grandchildren pictures of the roundup with my horse and I in the background and tell them stories and who knows maybe they will want to go to one and participate too some day. So often people are so wrapped up in work that they forget that there is this big beautiful world out there and part of it is in their own back yard. Just take a few minutes to look around and see just what is out there. Take a chance, try out new things and enjoy all the wild life GOD has created, this is so much healthier for the mind and soul to playing video games or sitting in a dark gloomy house all day every day. I love watching the turkeys every spring try to win over their mate and the deer and elk drinking from the creek. I love seeing mountain goats climbing and antelope grazing. The most spectacular animal to watch is the bald eagle soaring over the trees and swooping down to catch a meal. There is so much wild life to see and enjoy. While outside walking around I was thinking about the upcoming Buffalo Round Up and this poem came to mind and I will get to go next year, this is my goal.

HOOVES OF THUNDER

My guy full of power and beauty
With hooves of grace they come thundering
Down the hill towards me
Kicking and jumping as they approach
With such grace and strength their muscles gleam
As the sunlight bounces from their bodies
Their manes and tails floating through the air it seems
Their pounding hooves coming closer and closer
I feel the earth shaking
Then suddenly it just stops
I feel their warm breath upon my face
I hear their hearts beating
As if pounding through their chest
I run my hands down their long soft necks
As they hug me with their warm soft muzzles
I often wonder how GOD made such a powerful beast
And yet so gentle as my guys seem to be

The Mighty Round Up

It's that time of year again
Where excitement and awe
just fill the air
We are early to rise
to saddle our horses
To set out and battle
those unknown forces
with that last drop of coffee
drank from our cups
We head out to the long awaited
Great buffalo roundup
As the sun rises
over the pasture before us
We all gather round
for a moment to pray
dear LORD keep our crew
and animals safe
While we do our job
on this beautiful day
With the buffalo still grazing
They haven't a clue
That today is the day
We will cut out a few
With our cinches tightened
Our horses ready to go
The roundup begins at a pace
Were manes and tails just flow

Not only the thundering hooves
Of our horses we hear
But the hooves of the bison
We feel pounding quite near
With the clouds of dust
Now covering our faces
Our trusty steeds have
Picked up their paces
thundering down over the hills
To the awaiting corrals
the men at the gates
are right in their places
I'm just so glad
none of those beasts
So big and stout
Decided to take a turn about
But I was ready just in case
As was my horse
for that big challenging race
now that the roundup
is winding down
we unsaddle our horses
for the feast that's abound
today was a good day
the good LORD kept us all safe
We will enjoy the rest
of this evening
At a much slower pace

I have written many poems for so many reasons and this past Father's Day I really wanted to do something special for my dad. I felt I owed him this. My step dad was always great to me and it was hard when he passed away. But that really got me to thinking how short life really is. I want to get to know my dad better and I want him to know the real me. Sometimes I think my family still see me as I was as a teenager. Like they say, your childhood mistakes will follow you through your life. But I am not that lost little girl any more. I am a different person and a professional at that. I have a respectable job and I am a funny, easy going person. I realized last year after spending time with my dad and step mother, that my dad has a big sense of humor and is a likeable guy. I now know where my sense of humor comes from. It took a lot of years for this part of me to shine through but now that it has I thank my dad for that gift. My dad has always been a bit distant with me. I am not sure if it's because I am a girl and he doesn't know how to relate to me. I just don't know why he is not the type of dad who shows affection or love through hugging and saying "I love you." I do know my family loves me and they are pleased with my choice for a husband. They love Carl and think he has been great husband for me. Sometimes I think they like him more than they like me but I am so glad they love this guy I love. We all have fun when we get together but talking to my dad comes as a struggle for me. I still don't know why this is. I have so many friends who have such close relationships with their dads and I get along great with their dads. So why is it so hard for me to talk to my own dad? I love my dad; he has always been my hero. I always admired him for the work he does and his racing skills. He would never complain or borrow from anyone. If he needed something he would build it or buy it. My dad built his first race car out of an old coop at the age of 16. This became his first short rail race car. Over the years he would change things on it, a little upgrade here and there and a bit of a tweaking here and there. The paint jobs were great. I remember when I was younger my step mom wanted me to follow her into the garage to show me the paint job he had just done. It was beautiful, black and shiny. On the back of the car in gold shiny letters were two rows of names. All my brothers and on top in the middle between the two rows of names was my name. Mom looked at me and said "See, he does love you." I just know I had a big grin on my face that day. My dad had always built his own trailers to haul his car in. I always thought they were factory built and bought. He one day replied, "Hell, no! Those fall apart. I build my own." They were always nice and enclosed trailers and yes, well built. Dad eventually had to sell the short rail race car and he now runs a long rail. He says the long rails vibrate less. Dad still races today at the age of 76. He says as long as he passes his physicals he will continue racing. When we were younger, Dad always took us to the races and our job was to fill up water jugs at the hydrant and pour the water on the back tires to cool them off after each race. Dad also had two mini bikes he tinkered around with.

One was orange and one blue. It was always a great day when he would pull those out of the garage and get them running for us to ride. Most of the time they would be upright, but not for long. They, too, were well built and are still around today. My dad has passed his trailer building skills down to my youngest brother. This past year he built a trailer to haul all the 4-wheelers and motor cross bikes on. It is a very nice trailer and well built. The boys and kids and one or two of the sister-in-laws go out camping and riding several times every year. My dad and step mom go too. Dad got tired of being left out when they would go off climbing hills on the two wheelers. So by golly he built his own motor cycle. This was the toughest roughest thing I'd ever seen. Talk about a cool bike. Dad says it will climb anything in its path. Now it's always a race between the boys and my dad to the top of any hill. Dad decided my step mom could just keep riding the old 4-wheeler since he has his own bike to ride. I know when I am on the 4-wheeler here at home its always working or moving cattle. It would be nice to go camping and just play around some day with the family. My dad is so very talented; I am glad he is still able to do the things he enjoys. I just hope the poem I wrote for his Father's Day card this year will help us both to open up and we can have that relationship my heart needs. I love you Dad.

My dad can build most anything
Even with a piece of string
My dad built his own race car
My dad you will never
find in a bar
My dad not once but twice
could have died
But not one tear
did he ever cry
My dad loves to camp
and motor bike
Someday I hope we
can go fishing for pike
My dad has eight sons and
one daughter to boot
So Don't ask to borrow money
He's a bit short on loot
My dad has won many a race
I like to see that smile
upon his face
My dad is not one to say
I love you

He shows us by helping
with projects we do
My dad is not your average dad
But he's my hero and I am glad

I LOVE YOU DAD,

I have two sons: Brandon is my oldest at 36 years old and Jacob is 30. Brandon is currently employed at a big factory and is a part time student. Brandon has always been a good student and has a brilliant mind. Brandon has blessed us with seven grandchildren: two grandsons and five granddaughters. Some of the grandchildren are biological and some he has adopted but we don't treat any of the children different from the others and neither does he. Brandon has a busy household but loves and cares for all his children. Brandon and his fiancé have both had their fair share of misfortunes thrown at them throughout the years and they have always been best friends and helped each other out. They have always been there for one another. Brandon has always had a love for cooking. He loves cooking and inventing new recipes both on the stove and on the grill. Brandon has always been healthy food conscious. Everything he cooks with has to be fresh. He loves to stay healthy and goes to the gym every day after the kids go to school. Brandon does attend college and his goal is to become a licensed dietitian and a personal trainer on the side. His main goal is to get a job where he works days and can spend more time with his children. He loves the outdoors and likes to take the kids fishing and camping. He involves the kids in helping with the meals if they want to help and talks to them about good eating habits and bad eating habits. He listens to the kids about school and helps them with their homework. Every day book bags are checked for homework, notes or past school work. Brandon was able to accomplish one of his goals Sept. 2015. He has always wanted to run in The Spartan Race. This particular year it was held up by Chicago so I helped him fulfill his goal. He ran a good race and finished 95th in his group of 250. He is hoping next time this race is close enough to go to that he fiancé and maybe one or two of the older kids could also attend. Brandon is the most awesome father to all his children; I just wish more fathers were like him. The women who are the mothers of his children should all be thankful he is the type of dad he is and takes care of all their needs. This young man is no dead beat dad. Everything Brandon does or has done is to better himself so he can give his kids a better life and future. I am proud of you son.

Jacob lives out here in the same state that we live in. He is currently living up by the hills, and works outdoors and loves cutting trees down to make room for healthier ones to grow. They clear up slash piles and cut diseased or dead trees down and burn them. He also works at a saw mill and drives tractors to move piles of ready to sell bundles of posts. Jacob, like his brother, has always loved food and loves to cook. Jacob has a talent for art and is also a very intelligent young man. Jacob wrestled in elementary school. During high school Jacob played football and basketball. Jacob graduated in 2007 and moved to Wyoming and worked as a line man putting up power lines; he really succeeded in that job and really loved it until the work dried up. Jacob comes out to the ranch every year to camp and goes hunting. He keeps everything he hunts; this is what feeds him all winter. He grows a big garden with his dad and they freeze and can fresh vegetables. Jacob would like to someday become a smoke jumper but classes are far more than he can afford at this time. He loves the outdoors and fishes every chance he gets. He and his girlfriend Hailey live together and she goes to art school and this fall she will earn her degree. This young lady carries a 4.0 average, and hopes someday to become an art teacher or a graphic designer. Hailey is the lovely young lady who has graced the cover of my book with her unwavering talent. My sons have both made me a very proud mother. I have never once told them they would never amount to anything. I have always encouraged them and told them they have my full support in anything they do in life. And they have proven me right. Both boys have never been afraid to work. They are both fit and athletic and bright young men. They are both very handsome and have grown up as Christians. I will always be proud to point them out and say, "That's my son." I wrote one poem after Jacob left home to join the working world. I have learned to live with the empty nest syndrome but his bedroom and bathroom have never been changed and any time he comes home for a weekend he still uses his own bedroom. It's never easy turning your children out in the world and worrying about them never goes away. I always call them my baby boys; whether they are thirty or eighty years old they will always be my little boys. I am proud of how they have each turned out and I would not change anything about either one. I might want my oldest to live closer, but as I have said before, you have to live where the jobs are. So as I write this book I realize I have two very talented young men who are working and are contributing members of society. Who could ask for more?

Love Through Tears

I miss you son
Like you'll never know
The summer has left us
The snow will soon blow
With the bite of winter
that will be in the air
My body will chill
While my heart tries to bear
The seasons keep changing
As they come and they go
But your mother's love
will continue to grow
The wind has begun shaking
these now browned leaves
From their cold homes
that once were these trees
The birds have stopped singing
as they shiver from the cold
As I sit here in the warmth
I wonder how I got so old
My tears will dry up
again you will see
Just as the leaves will
turn green on these trees

the birds will sing yet
another new song
and you will be home to visit
I know it won't be too long

Greatest Joys

My dearest son you're like no other
Except that you're tall and handsome
Just like your brother
Your minds so quick and pencil sharp
I knew you were special
Right from the very start
You're so artistic
And good with your hands
The artwork you produce
Is all just grand
With time you've grown
so responsible and bright
You are my sons
my shining lights
My two sons my greatest joys
They both enjoy
those big boy toys
They live what seems
like worlds apart
So much alike
and dear to my heart

Out of all my brothers I could without a doubt say I am closest to my older brother Robert. Randy and Robert are the oldest and a set of twins. The reason I say Robert and I are closest is during my struggles as a teenager and young mom, Robert and I lived together on several occasions. During my young teenage drinking years, Robert always made sure I was ok when I would come home from drinking way too much. I would go to his apartment instead going to my mother and I's apartment and having to face my mom. I guess you could say he hid me from my stupidity. Robert had also more times than once moved from Arizona to home and each time I opened my home to him as he had done for me. We always got along and Robert is the most laid back easy going guy I know aside from my husband. Whenever I would have a down day I could call Robert and he would come by or come and get me and take me back to where he would be working and set me at a table with something to eat and a soda. Robert would do his job and take care of me also. I ran away from a home when I was 15 and hitched a ride with friends to Texas. I was there the whole summer living life to the fullest until I became sick. I caught an intestinal bug and felt I needed to go back home. My oldest son's dad and I hitch our way back home and catching a ride. An older man in his late sixties picked us up and offered us up a ride to Oklahoma. He invited us to stay awhile at his house until I felt well enough to travel on. Little did I know he too had other plans. After staying with this man a couple days he sent my boy friend to the store knowing he would be gone awhile; so he decided to just slip into bed next to me. I knew I could fight off an old man but instead I became frigid and asked him just what was he doing? He said he thought I might want to pay him back for his hospitality. I told him I was unaware I had to pay him in this manner and to get out. I pushed him out of the bed and I got up and ran outside. I ran until I found a phone booth and I called my brother Robert to please come get me. The next day my brother was there to give me a ride home. I love him so much for that. Robert has always been there when I needed him. The year my Grandpa H. passed away and I rode down to Florida with my mom, dad and Robert, we talked quite a bit in the back seat and spent time walking through the mall while Grandpa was sleeping or giving other family time to be with him. Robert and I can talk about anything I guess, except for my past. I finally told him this past summer about my past and about writing this book. He was shocked to say the least but is also proud at how well I turned out. He agreed I easily could have been a drug addict or alcoholic. I chose to be a mother and the best one I could be. And the best sister a brother could have. I mainly wanted to prove to several of my family members who saw me as the person I was not, that I am a good person. I was not a sexual vixen and was not a pot head. I was actually the total opposite. I tried smoking pot but I got nothing out of it except headaches. And sex was the last thing on my mind. My brothers turned out to be the best brothers a sister could have. So when Robert had a knee replacement last year I sent him a card and what good is a card without a good funny poem inside. Robert loves humor and that's what I like about him.

The Healthy Knee

I heard you had a surgery
I'm thinking it was on your knee
When you went to your doctor
Just what did he see
Was it your left knee
Or this time the right
Did this happen at work
Or at home during the night
Did you happen to fall
While walking down
the hall
Or when you turned to sit down
Did it get twisted all wrong
When seeing your doctor
did you sing
your favorite song
It's too bad you're now stuck
Just sitting at home
Most days you know
You will spend primarily alone
Just be thankful you have
Your healthy middle knee
For all those irritating times
You will need to painfully get up
JUST TO GO PEE

After moving out to the ranch, life was finally getting better for all of us. Carl and I were working well together and I was learning a lot about ranch life and how to run most of the machinery. I found windrowing was my favorite chore to do. I really enjoyed the solitude of being out in the field cutting alfalfa hay. This is the best smell in the world: the freshly cut alfalfa and the blooms. I had plenty of time to think and enjoyed seeing the difference I was making. During these times of solitude I wrote a lot of my poems. I always had a pencil with me and a pad of paper. One poem I enjoyed writing was my wedding poem. I had been planning my wedding with the help of several friends. I never thought I would ever get married again or would trust another man to marry. Carl, from the day I met him, was not just any man. I had a good feeling or vibe you could say about him. I can say I trusted him when at this time in my life I trusted nobody. He had a kindness about him that few people have. I could tell right off that he had a gentle presence about him and I could trust my gut. I went with my gut feeling and I was right. After two years of living and working together we decided to get married. I should say, after my mom talked with Carl one day on the phone (this was their first meeting) she decided we should get married. My mom, still 800 miles away, had that same feeling about Carl. She told me he had a nice voice and she felt he was a good man. I never thought I would hear my mom say that about anyone she just met over the phone. I believed it when a month later I received the most beautiful wedding dress in the mail from my mom. I opened that box up and laughed. I told Carl I think we are going to get married. A year later we were married. It was a long winter and spring getting prepared for this wedding. I wanted everything I could to be handmade. So with the help of friends and neighbors we set out to make bridesmaid dresses in the same design as my wedding dress and the flowers I picked out we made into bouquets and boutonnieres. During this time we had good times and bad times as the sewing and such went on. We spent many evenings up at the Walters's home sewing, and cutting and flower making. In doing so I spent many a day in the field writing about it. I wanted everything to be perfect. This would be my dream wedding. I was going to have my dad walk me down the aisle. This would be the most wonderful day of my life. So I thought. It was still the greatest day but my dad would not be walking me down the aisle as I thought he would. He was in a bad wreck. He and my stepmother Judy were on their way to Indiana for a race when they came upon road construction. Everyone was stopped and waiting except a semi who was coming up behind Dad's trailer with the dragster in it. The semi driver forgot he was to stop also and hit the trailer and causing an explosive train reaction. My dad and mom were both wearing seat belts but somehow the back of her seat busted and it laid her in a supine position and during this moment she was knocked unconscious. My dad got himself out of the suburban and ran around the vehicle to get mom out. The trailer and suburban were both engulfed in flames by this time. Dad could not get in so he tried the driver's side again. There was no getting through his door. In order to save her, he went back to her side of the vehicle and fought through the flames and rescued her. They both had God looking out for them. There was a 5 gallon jug of water behind Mom's seat; this jug is all that was saving Mom from being burned by those flames. My stepmom did suffer from some burns which she received while dad was getting her out and she had some badly bruised ribs and a concussion. Dad was badly burned and is once again a hero in my eyes. He was unable to attend the wedding to walk me down the aisle but I understood; I knew he could not risk infection. My stepmom came out with my brother Randy and his family. She said she would not have missed it for the world. I had to quickly figure out who would walk me down the aisle though. My second choice was easy, I thought. I really wanted my stepdad to do the honors but was thinking how this might hurt my dad feelings. So I thought why not give this honor to all my brothers. After all Robert has no children so he will never walk a daughter down the aisle, Paul has all boys so no walking down an aisle for him. So I decided my brothers should do me the honors. My step brothers were unable to attend and my brother Matthew had just started at a new job so could not get off. But my brothers, the twins Randy and Robert, and my brothers Jacob and Paul all walked me down the aisle. I am happy with that choice. I did dance the father daughter dance with my step dad. I picked out songs for my wedding that had special meaning to me. The father daughter dance was to "Daddy's Hands." I walked down the aisle to a friend, Mary, singing the song" From This Moment". I now cry every time I hear that song. These tears are however happy tears. We have now been married going on 18 years. These have been the best 18 years of my life. I have nothing but love and admiration for my wonderful and patient husband. He has taught me so much about how to take life one day at a time and how to not sweat the little things. I now take time to smell all the flowers. I used to suffer from bad migraines but those, too, have gone. I enjoy life to the fullest and get all I can out of the love from him and my animals. Nothing is more loving than a dog and there are no better kisses than those from a lovable old cow. I guess you could say it would be more of a sliming than a kiss I have found out from experience. But my Darla cow is a great old lovable girl. To just be able to walk outside and wrap your arms around the neck of one of my horses and breathe in the smell of that wonderful animal is great. It is a dream come true to be surrounded by so much of GODS wonderful creatures and the man of my dreams. I could never love anyone like I love him. Now I will always trust my gut.

Pre Wedding Trials

We all had our good days
And some of us our bad
But we all stuck together, and I am so glad
We are so blessed to have such family and friends
To help us see this day to the end
We just can't come up with enough words
To express our gratitude and thanks you see
So I wrote this poem from us, Mr. and Mrs. To be

It all started at the Big Rays
When he walked in, for a moment to stay
With the exchange of a glance, and a couple smiles
That's all it took to travel those thirty five miles
I came to see him, and he came to see me
This turned into love that will always be
A couple of years had quickly gone by
As we worked together side by side
He then asked me to be his wife
I answered "yes"
With you would be a great life
So now you know how it all began
The rest is how the wedding was planned

You have to admit there was a lot of fussin
With Harold and Carl doing most of the cussin
There was an awful lot that had to be done

But we also took time to make it all fun
I kept asking myself "where did the time go"
I came to the conclusion
the same place as the cash flow
We weren't alone in this battle by far
We had family and friends and the little blue car
There was Misty, Lynn, Ruth, Evelyn and Frank you see
Oh boy what a circus that first night turned out to be
We all got together at the Walters household
For flowers to be made as the weather turned cold
Soon came the rain then all of this snow
The roads turned to ice don't we all know
But we made bouquets out of all those flowers
They were so beautiful and the hit of the hour
Frank fixed dinner for all of us girls
We ate like horses and scurried about like squirrels
The little blue car sat out in the drive
Slowly but surely just up and died
The phone call I dreaded but had to make
Knowing Carl and Jacob it would surely awake
The two of the came to my rescue and aid
On those roads of ice that the rain had made
The dresses I know were a lot Misty
I could have flushed them
right down the latrine
When the day came for the dresses to be made
We all got together for our talents to trade
Frank ran to the city for needles and chicks
And would return home lickety-split
The serger we needed to complete all of our dresses
Without the needles we just pinned

And cut and made many messes
The weather decided to turn very sour
Poor Evelyn had been pacing for well over an hour
"Will Frank make it home on these roads of ice?"
How could this happen, not once, but twice?
We all got to worrying about ol' Frank you know
Then out the window we saw his headlights a glow
Oh, what a relief that was for us all
To see Frank, the needles, and baby chicks
were so small
The dresses we made and oh how they flowed
With Pam's help that night
The girls just all glowed
The invitations arrived and had to be mailed
From the post office we would send them
At the pace of a snail
Somehow I knew this would be quite a chore
So I enlisted some help, and I got help galore
We folded and stuffed, addressed and stamped
At Martha's dining room table
We all just camped
Misty got a phone call and said "we must go"
Fog was moving in thick,
Driving would surely be slow
Now rice bags we knew just had to be made
Using bird seed instead
We felt was a good trade
Misty and I enlisted the help of Lou Anne
The making of these bags slowly began
The tulle we cut out,
The bird seed we scooped

When this chore was all finished
I think we were pooped
The Hershey Kiss bags were last to be made
Then all was done
And to rest could be laid
At Martha's we met
Misty and I running late
The kisses wrapped in foil
Shadow dog thought they were great
The rest is just little things
That needs to be done
None of it near the enjoyment
Nor half of the fun
So now I shall end this poem for you
With my family so far
This joyous time would have been blue
Thanks to Carls family and so many friends
It has all been done and happily ends

Thankful For You

As the holiday seasons drawn near
Our hearts and minds will glow
We think of friends and family
God and gifts and snow
But this year will be different
At least it will for me
For there are things I am thankful for
That I have never seen
Many things have changed for me
All good no bad it's true
The things I'm most thankful for
Have come to me through you
Thank you for the sunshine
That you bring to me each day
Even when it's stormy out
You chase the clouds away
Thank you for your kindness
And your patience every day
Thank you for the love you share
That never goes away
Thank you for enlightening me
When life seems so very mean
You've been so strong for both of us
On you I have had to lean

You held us up through struggles
Through many tears and strife
But most of all I thank you Carl
For giving me back my life

After writing this book I lost my sweet dear Grandma. She was my life and our matriarch. I am not sure as to how long it will take to recover from this loss but I know I will make it through. I still have my sweet dog Dalia along with my husband and animals here on the ranch, so I will get by. I miss my grandma dearly and was just thankful that I decided at the moment I heard she was in the hospital, to drop everything to go home and be with her. I was able to write a poem for her, too, but was not given the time to say a proper good-bye with this poem at her funeral. Sometimes I have learned family can hurt you more when you are hurting already. There have been some hurt feelings from this due to one grandson being allowed to sing, not one, but two songs and two of the three granddaughters not being allowed to speak at all. I will say my good-bye in this book. I know my grandmother and I had a very close and special bond and the love I had for her will never die. Grandma, it is only because of you I have overcame all my hardships and abuse and have had the strength and courage to speak about it and write this book. Your wisdom, love and guidance have been my beacon of light through some of my darkest days. I love you, Grandma, and I know you will be at those pearly gates waiting to hug me.

Grandma's Hands

Grandma's hands were always busy
Whether fixing a meal
Or painting a picture
how they look so real
It never mattered how busy she was
Grandma always had time
to pass out the hugs
whether she was cooking or cleaning
or painting beautiful landscapes or roses
she would take time to wipe
our many runny noses
If we had a tear running down
Our dirty cheeks or a
Skinned up knee needing cleaned
Grandma was always there
With a tissue in hand
Or a band-aid to please
Grandma never sat still
For very long
There were always chores
To be done
And the many errands
Needing to be run
With her hands
Always at the ready
And her legs to keep her
At a pace so steady

Grandma was able to nurse
Her many patients back to health
With GOD guiding her beautiful hands
This was Grandmas greatest wealth
We admire our Grandma
Our Grandma the nurse
Who could pull snacks and
Band-aids magically from her purse
Grandma now has slowed down
As if it happened over night
Her hands now weakened
the pain not slight
so delicate and frail
her legs no longer strong
have some managed to fail
she knows it won't be long
the LORD has come
to take her home
the time has come for Grandma to go
I pray she was not alone
Instead surrounded by her family
For her hands they all would hold
With her she will take
A life time of wonderful memories
While leaving behind
Her family in tears
And many untold stories
Throughout her past years

Printed in the United States
By Bookmasters

Printed in the United States
By Bookmasters